THE **AMOT** GUIDE TO

Military Museums
in the UK

2010/11 Edition

A visitor's guide to over 140 museums in
England, Scotland, Wales and Northern Ireland,
produced by the **Army Museums Ogilby Trust**

The AMOT Guide to Military Museums in the UK

Copyright © 2010 Army Museums Ogilby Trust

First published in 2007 by Third Millennium Publishing Limited.

Second edition published 2010 by Third Millennium Publishing Limited,
a subsidiary of Third Millennium Information Limited,
2–5 Benjamin Street, London EC1M 5QL, United Kingdom

www.tmiltd.com

ISBN 978 1 906507 51 0

Produced by Third Millennium Publishing,
a subsidiary of Third Millennium Information Limited

Designed by Matthew Wilson
Edited by Colin Sibun
Production by Bonnie Murray

Reprographics by Studio Fasoli, Italy
Printed by Gorenjski Tisk, Slovenia

Contents

Foreword

by

His Royal Highness The Duke of York KG, KCVO, ADC

BUCKINGHAM PALACE

Military museums across the country are a rich source of historical information and they provide unique insights into the inspirational deeds of courage, bravery and good humoured fortitude that have characterised the British Army through the centuries.

The Army Museums Ogilby Trust was established to safeguard the principal feature which its founder believed distinguished the British Army from all others, and that was the fighting spirit that its soldiers drew from the regimental system. At a time of change and reorganisation, when the identities of famous old regiments become blurred by amalgamation and new ones take their place, the museums described in this Guide ensure that the golden thread of Britain's military heritage is preserved for the Nation and made accessible to the public.

Regimental and Corps museums, together with the prestigious National museums also listed in this Guide, form a network that stretches throughout the United Kingdom. Often taking their character from the communities that provide their soldiers, they can impose a local perspective on their portrayal of events of national importance. In addition to the collections that are so proudly displayed, most of them possess valuable archive material and many provide modern, interactive displays to educate and entertain. They have something of interest for all from Old Comrades to the adventurous young and from the serious student of military history to the casual visitor.

As Patron of the Army Museums Ogilby Trust, I have no hesitation in warmly recommending a visit to each and every one of the museums in this Guide.

Introduction

The 2nd edition of this popular publication by the Army Museums Ogilby Trust (AMOT) is the only comprehensive listing of military museums in the United Kingdom and is approved by the Ministry of Defence as the definitive guide to the regimental and corps museums of the British Army. Building on the work of Terrence and Shirley Wise first published in 1969, this updated version has been produced in conjunction with Third Millennium Publishing whose generous support and expert professional help have once more made it all possible.

The Army Museums Ogilby Trust is a registered charity founded in 1954 by Colonel Robert Ogilby to support and promote the regimental and corps museums of the British Army. This Guide is a natural extension of that role and complements the Trust's website www.armymuseums.org.uk, which not only lists all the museums but includes useful advice on ancestor research and regimental bibliographies for genealogists and military historians.

For the convenience of the visitor the museums are shown in 13 regional sections, each with its own accompanying map. All the museums reflect strong regimental pride and individuality and provide a unique portrayal of life in their own regiments. Items such as the bugle that sounded the charge at the Battle of Balaclava, Eagle standards captured from Napoleon's armies, the first tanks and early military aircraft and the keys to the City of Corunna have pride of place alongside colourful displays of uniforms, badges, medals and weapons that trace military history through the ages. Rich in artefacts and information, the items on display are often augmented by comprehensive regimental archives which are a treasure trove for military historians and those researching their military ancestors.

Family history research can be complicated by the numerous changes that have affected regimental titles. Towards the back of the Guide is a Succession of Titles section containing simple tables which enable the reader to trace the identity of a particular regiment or corps from its title in the 1881 Army List right through to the most recent round of regimental amalgamations in 2006/7.

Overleaf is more information about the Army Museums Ogilby Trust and its activities on behalf of regimental and corps museums. Advice is also provided for those wishing to help safeguard the Nation's proud military heritage by making a personal contribution to support the Trust's work.

Colin Sibun
Director
Army Museums Ogilby Trust
October 2010

The Army Museums Ogilby Trust

The Trust is a registered charity founded in 1954 by the late Colonel Robert Ogilby DSO DL whose personal experiences in two world wars persuaded him that the fighting spirit of the British soldier stemmed from the *esprit de corps* fostered by the Army's regimental structure. In accordance with his vision this spirit is enshrined in the many regimental and corps museums which seek to inspire and educate their visitors.

Its underlying objectives remain those set by its founder, adapted and developed to encourage a contemporary presentation of military heritage geared to the education of young people by reference to the national curriculum and reflecting the changing needs of regimental and corps museums. Currently the Trust supports museums in the following ways:

- With the agreement of their trustees, to represent the individual and collective views of regimental and corps museums and to champion their cause in dealings with the Ministry of Defence, other government departments and their agencies.

- Through close liaison with the Ministry of Defence, the Museums, Libraries and Archives Council, National Army Museum, the Charity Commissioners and other professional agencies, to track developments in policy and practise and to pass that information to regimental and corps museums through regular conferences, newsletters and strategy papers.

- The provision of free legal and specialist advice and assistance with the constitution, structure and registration of existing and projected museums, including the creation of new trusts to embrace the collections of several pre-existing museums.

- Securing – in conjunction with other agencies – the best available advice on such professional matters as the protection, conservation, preservation and presentation of their collections, and the operation and further development of their museums.

- The provision of a website, approved by the Ministry of Defence, as the definitive guide to regimental and corps museums.

- Participation in the development of Ministry of Defence policy towards museums to ensure that the interests and concerns of museum trustees are properly represented, thereby ensuring the best possible future for regimental and corps museums.

The British Army has a rich history that is added to continually as today's soldiers perpetuate the proud traditions of their regimental forebears. Their museums record this history and portray the achievements and development of the Army as a whole. The Trust assists such museums with funds, advocacy, information and advice. Its income is derived solely from donations and bequests and it would warmly welcome gifts, legacies or covenants from those who support its views and objectives.

Should you wish to:

MAKE A DONATION, however small, it would be most gratefully received by the AMOT Director at this address:

Army Museums Ogilby Trust
58, The Close, Salisbury, Wiltshire SP1 2EX

CONSIDER A LEGACY, there is further information and a suitable form of words on our website www.armymuseums.org.uk

Your generosity could have a profound impact on the preservation of the nation's military heritage

WARNING

All details of opening hours and admission prices are correct at the time of publication, but these do change from time to time and visitors are strongly encouraged to contact museums before making a visit.

Part I

Regimental and Corps Museums

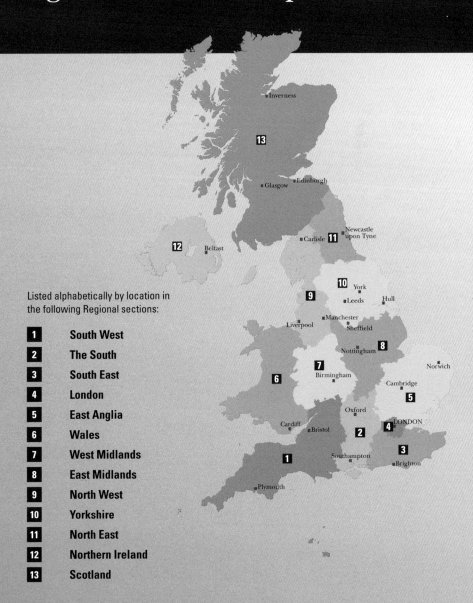

Listed alphabetically by location in
the following Regional sections:

South West

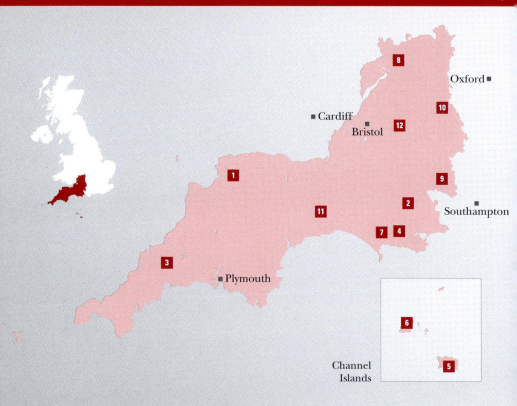

Barnstaple:	1	Royal Devon Yeomanry Museum Collection
Blandford Forum:	2	Royal Signals Museum
Bodmin:	3	Cornwall's Regimental Museum
Bovington:	4	The Tank Museum
Channel Islands:	5	Royal Guernsey Light Infantry and Militia Museum
	6	Jersey Militia Museum
Dorchester:	7	The Keep Military Museum
Gloucester:	8	Soldiers of Gloucestershire Museum
Salisbury:	9	The Rifles (Berkshire and Wiltshire) Museum
Swindon:	10	Royal Wiltshire Yeomanry Collection
Taunton:	11	Somerset Military Museum
Warminster:	12	Infantry and Small Arms School Corps Weapons Collection

Barnstable

ROYAL DEVON YEOMANRY MUSEUM COLLECTION

Museum situated in the town centre near the clock tower on the square at the end of Long Bridge. A short walk from bus and railway stations. By road, follow signs to town centre from the North Devon Link Road

Museum of Barnstaple and North Devon
The Square, Barnstaple,
Devonshire EX32 8LN
T: 01271 346747 / F: 01271 346407
E: Alison.Mills@northdevon.gov.uk
www.devonmuseums.net/barnstaple

Curator: Alison Mills

Royal Devon Yeomanry, Royal 1st Devon Yeomanry, North Devon Yeomanry Hussars

The regimental collections of the yeomanry regiments of Devon from 1794 to the present day. Access to the regimental archive is available by appointment. The collection is an outstation of The Keep Military Museum in Dorchester.

Opening Hours: Mon–Fri 9.30am–5pm

Admission: Free. Groups and school parties by arrangement

Facilities: Toilets, shop, disabled access to ground floor

Blandford Forum

ROYAL SIGNALS MUSEUM

Approximately 4 miles northwest of Blandford Forum on the A350

Royal Signals Museum, Blandford Camp,
Blandford Forum, Dorset DT11 8RH
T: 01258 482248 / F: 01258 482084
E: info@royalsignalsmuseum.com
http://www2.armynet.mod.uk/museums/royalsignals.com

Director: Nick Kendall-Carpenter
Curator: Tina Pittock

Royal Corps of Signals, Royal Signals, Royal Engineers Signal Service, Royal Engineers Telegraphs

The collection reflects the history of military communications from the Crimea to the present day with displays on the Great War, World War II, Korea, the Falklands and the Gulf War. There is reference to the activities of the Special Operations Executive (SOE), the ATS, Long Range Desert Group and SAS Signals featuring vehicles, motorbikes, uniforms, medals, equipment, memorabilia and trench art. It addresses the history of codes and code-breaking. The museum has a variety of excellent interactive displays with competitions and 'fun trails' to appeal to the younger visitor. The Corps library and archive are on-site and may be viewed by appointment. Research facilities are available.

Opening Hours: Mon–Fri 10am–5pm
Bank Holidays and weekends Feb–Oct: 10am–4pm
Closed Christmas and New Year

Admission: Adults £7.50, Seniors £6.50, Children (5–16 years) £5.50, Family ticket £22. Groups and school parties by arrangement

Facilities: Car and coach parking, restaurant, toilets, lecture room, shop, disabled access, picnic area. No dogs (except guide dogs)

Bodmin

CORNWALL'S REGIMENTAL MUSEUM 3

Approximately 0.25 miles south of town centre on B3269

Cornwall's Regimental Museum
The Keep, Bodmin, Cornwall PL31 1EG
T: 01208 72810 / F: 01208 72810
E: dclimus@talk21.com

Curator: Major Trevor Stipling

The Light Infantry and all antecedent regiments of the Light Infantry. Somerset and Cornwall Light Infantry, 32nd (Cornwall) Light Infantry, 32nd (or the Cornwall) Regiment of Foot, Colonel Fox's Regiment of Marines, 46th (South Devonshire) Regiment of Foot, 46th (or South Devonshire) Regiment of Foot, 46th Regiment of Foot, Colonel Price's Regiment of Foot

The museum and regimental archive are housed in a listed Militia building built in 1859 at the time of the Napoleonic threat. From raising the regiment in 1702 and the capture of Gibraltar in 1704 the museum covers the history of the County Regiment through the amalgamation in 1959 to form The Light Infantry until the formation of The Rifles in 2007. It houses the collections of the DCLI, the LI and the Volunteers in the County. Exhibits include weapons, medals, insignia, uniforms, pictures, George Washington's Bible, which was captured by the 46th Foot in 1777, up to modern displays which include a mortar base plate used by the IRA and the largest section of the Berlin Wall in the Country.

Opening Hours: Mon–Fri 9am–5pm, Sun (Jul and Aug only) 10am–4pm

Admission: Adults/Seniors £2, children 50p, groups/school parties by arrangement

Facilities: Car and coach parking, toilets, lecture room, shop, some disabled access. Refreshments adjacent

Bovington

THE TANK MUSEUM 4

Bovington Camp is approximately 8 miles from Wareham and two miles from Wool, which is the nearest railway station. There is a bus and taxi service from Wool

The Tank Museum, Bovington Camp,
Dorset BH20 6JG
T: 01929 405096 / F: 01929 405360
E: admin@tankmuseum.co.uk
www.tankmuseum.co.uk

Director: Richard Smith

Royal Armoured Corps, Royal Tank Regiment, Royal Tank Corps, Tank Corps

The Tank Museum houses the most comprehensive collection of armoured vehicles in the world. It tells the story of tanks and armoured warfare illustrated through scientific and technological developments, woven together with stories of human endeavour on the battlefield. An extensive archive and library may be viewed by appointment. See the website for School Holiday and Special Events. All visitors receive an Annual Pass at no extra cost.

Opening Hours: Daily 10am–5pm.
Closed Christmas (from 21–26 Dec) and New Year's Day

Admission: Adults £11, Seniors £9, Children £7.50 (5–16 years). Children under 16 years MUST be accompanied by an adult. Family ticket s £30 (2 adults + 2 children), £27 (1 adult + 3 children)

Facilities: Car/coach parking, toilets, restaurant, shop, disabled access, lecture room

Channel Islands

JERSEY MILITIA MUSEUM

Jersey Militia Museum Collection
Elizabeth Castle, St Aubin's Bay,
St Helier, Jersey JE2 3NF
T: 01534 833135
F: 01534 833101
E. museum@jerseyheritagetrust.org
www.jerseyheritagetrust.org

Head of Archives and Collections:
Linda Romeril

A small collection of objects associated with the Jersey Militia and the military history of the island.

Opening Hours: Daily 10am–6pm. Last admission 5pm

Admission: Adults £8.50, Seniors £7.50, Children £6, Family ticket £15.40. Groups and school parties by appointment

Facilities: Parking, toilets, refreshments, shop, disabled access

ROYAL GUERNSEY LIGHT INFANTRY AND MILITIA MUSEUM

Within Castle Cornet

Royal Guernsey Light Infantry and Militia Collections
Castle Cornet, St Peter Port
Guernsey GY1 1AU
T: 01481 721657 / F: 01481 714021
E: matt.harvey@cultureleisure.gov.gg
F: www.museum.guernsey.net

Social History Curator: Matt Harvey

Royal Guernsey Light Infantry Regimental Museum:
A gallery opened in 2009 tells of the formation of the RGLI during World War I, with displays of uniforms, medals, posters and weapons. The part played by the regiment in the Battle of Cambrai, 1917, is depicted in a diorama and in audio recordings of soldiers' diaries. A small research station allows visitors access to the photographic archive and other material.

Royal Guernsey Militia Regimental Museum: A gallery due to open in autumn 2010 follows the Militia from its foundation in the fourteenth century through to 1939. Incorporating parts of the Spencer Collection, displays include uniforms, weapons, badges, medals, standards and band instruments.

Both galleries are located within Castle Cornet which also houses the 201 Squadron (RAF) Museum, The Maritime Museum and The Story of Castle Cornet.

Dorchester

THE KEEP MILITARY MUSEUM

At the western edge of Dorchester, near the Top o' the Town roundabout on the A35

The Keep Military Museum,
Bridport Road,
Dorchester DT1 1RN
T: 01305 264066 / F: 01305 250373
E: curator@keepmilitarymuseum.org
www.keepmilitarymuseum.org

Curator: Captain Colin A Parr

Devonshire and Dorset Regiment, Devonshire Regiment, 11th (or North Devonshire) Regiment of Foot, 11th Regiment of Foot, Duke of Beaufort's Musketeers, Dorset Regiment, 39th (or Dorsetshire) Regiment of Foot, 39th (or East Middlesex) Regiment of Foot, 39th Regiment of Foot, Colonel Richard Coote's Regiment of Foot, 54th (or West Norfolk) Regiment of Foot, 54th Regiment of Foot, 56th Regiment of Foot, Queen's Own Dorset Yeomanry, Dorset Yeomanry, Dorset Militia, Royal Dorset Yeomanry, 94 Field Regiment Royal Artillery

The collections of the regiments of Devon and Dorset, including Volunteer and Militia units, from 1685 to the present day. Touch-screen computers, videos and displays tell of the courage, humour and self sacrifice of the soldiers and their families who have served the County Regiments of Devon and Dorset over 300 years. The museum offers wonderful rooftop views as well.

If you are a UK taxpayer, you can Gift Aid your admission fee and receive a year's free annual membership in return.

Opening Hours: Apr–Sep: Mon–Sat 9.30am–5pm. Bank Holidays 10am–4pm. Closed Sun. Oct–Mar: Tue–Sat 10am–4.30pm. Closed Sat, Sun and Mon. Last admission 1 hour before closing.

Admission: Adults £6, Seniors £4, Children (8–16 years) £2.50, Family ticket £14. Groups and school parties by appointment

Facilities: Parking, toilets, refreshments, shop, disabled access, picnic area

Gloucester

SOLDIERS OF GLOUCESTERSHIRE MUSEUM

A 10-minute walk from the city centre, following brown signs to the Historic Docks

Soldiers of Gloucestershire Museum,
Custom House, Gloucester Docks,
Gloucester GL1 2HE
T: 01452 522682 / F: 01452 31116
E: enquiries@sogm.co.uk
www.glosters.org.uk

Curator: Major George Streatfeild

Royal Gloucestershire, Berkshire and Wiltshire Regiment, Gloucestershire Regiment, 28th (or North Gloucestershire) Regiment of Foot, 28th Regiment of Foot, Colonel Gibson's Regiment of Foot, 61st (or South Gloucestershire) Regiment of Foot, 61st Regiment of Foot, 3rd Foot (2nd Battalion) re-constituted as 61st Foot, Royal Gloucestershire Hussars

The collections of the Regiments of Gloucestershire accumulated over the last 300 years. Exciting and colourful displays include life-sized dioramas, sound effects, archive film and many interesting exhibits reflecting the history of the County's regiments in the service of the Crown. The library and archive of the Gloucestershire Regiment are housed nearby and may be viewed by appointment.

Opening Hours: Jun–Sep: Daily 10am–5pm. Oct–May: Closed on Sundays

Admission: Adults £4.25, Seniors/Students/Concessions £3.25, Children £2.25, Family ticket (2+2) £13. Groups and school parties by appointment

Facilities: Pay and Display parking, toilets, shop, disabled access

Salisbury

THE RIFLES (BERKSHIRE AND WILTSHIRE) MUSEUM

In the Cathedral Close, near the city centre and a 15-minute walk from bus and railway stations

The Rifles (Berkshire and Wiltshire) Museum,
58 The Close, Salisbury SP1 2EX
T: 01722 419419 / F: 01722 421626
E: curator@thewardrobe.org.uk
www.thewardrobe.org.uk

Manager and Curator: Michael Cornwell
Assistant Curator: Jackie Dryden

The Rifles, Royal Gloucestershire, Berkshire and Wiltshire Regiment, Duke of Edinburgh's Royal Regiment (Berkshire & Wiltshire), Royal Berkshire Regiment (Princess Charlotte of Wales's), Princess Charlotte of Wales's Berkshire Regiment, 49th Princess of Wales's Herefordshire Regiment of Foot, 49th Herefordshire Regiment of Foot, Colonel Edward Trelawney's Regiment of Foot, 49th (6th or Cotterell's Marines), 66th (Berkshire) Regiment of Foot, 66th Regiment of Foot, Wiltshire Regiment (Duke of Edinburgh's), 62nd (Wiltshire) Regiment of Foot, 62nd Regiment of Foot, 99th (The Duke of Edinburgh's) Regiment of Foot, 99th (Lanarkshire) Regiment of Foot, 99th (Jamaica) Regiment of Foot (disbanded), Volunteers and Militia

Housed on the ground floor of a fine medieval building with a well-stocked riverside garden, this collection covers the history of the County Regiments of Berkshire and Wiltshire and their more recent successors. The regimental library and archive are housed in the same building and may be viewed by appointment. There is an on-site licensed tearoom and restaurant called Bernieres, after the village on the Normandy coast where the 5th Battalion Royal Berkshires landed on D-Day.

Opening Hours: Apr–Oct: Open daily 10am–5pm.
Feb, Mar Nov: Closed Mon. Dec, Jan: Closed

Admission: Adults £3.50, Seniors/Students/Concessions £2.75, Children £1, Family ticket £8. Groups and schools £2 per head by appointment

Facilities: Toilets, restaurant, shop, disabled access, lecture room

Swindon

ROYAL WILTSHIRE YEOMANRY COLLECTION **10**

Royal Wiltshire Yeomanry Collection, A (RWY) Squadron Royal Yeomanry, Church Place, Swindon, Wiltshire SN1 5EH
T: 01793 523865
F: 01793 529350
www.swindon.gov.uk/ heritage-yeomanry

Curator: Captain Christopher Elliott

A small, private regimental collection covering all aspects of the Royal Wiltshire Yeomanry since its formation in 1794.

Opening Hours: By appointment

Admission: Free

Facilities: Parking, toilets

The regimental archive is held by Wiltshire and Swindon Archives Wiltshire and Swindon History Centre, Cocklebury Road, Chippenham, Wiltshire SN15 3QN

T: 01249 705500
E: archives@wiltshire.gov.uk

Taunton

SOMERSET MILITARY MUSEUM **11**

Located within the Museum of Somerset, in Taunton's town centre.

Somerset Military Museum, Museum of Somerset, Taunton Castle, Somerset TA1 4AA
T: 01823 333434
E: taunton@the-rifles.co.uk
www.sommilmuseum.org.uk

Curator: Lieutenant Colonel Mike Motum

The Rifles, Somerset and Cornwall Light Infantry, Somerset Light Infantry, Somerset Light Infantry (Prince Albert's), Prince Albert's (Somerset Light Infantry), Prince Albert's (Somersetshire Light Infantry), 13th or Prince Albert's Regiment of Light Infantry, 13th (or 1st Somersetshire) Regiment of Foot (Light Infantry), 13th (1st Somersetshire) Regiment of Foot, 13th Regiment of Foot,, Earl of Barrymore's Regiment of Foot (Pearce's Dragoons), The Earl of Huntingdon's Regiment of Foot, Somerset Militia, Somerset Rifle Volunteer Regiments, North Somerset Yeomanry, West Somerset Yeomanry.

A comprehensive and well displayed collection covering the history of the County Regiments of Somerset from 1685 and an explanation of how the former Yeomanry Regiments of Somerset combined with the Somerset Light Infantry Territorials to form an important element of today's Regiment, The Rifles. The coverage of The Somerset Light Infantry including the First Afghan War including the Siege of Jellalabad and an extensive medal gallery are of particular note. The Regimental archive of The Somerset Light Infantry and The North Somerset Yeomanry is held at the County Record Office but some archive material is held at The Rifles Office, 14 Mount Street, Taunton (Tel: 01823 333434). For details see website. Archive material may be viewed by appointment only. During the temporary closure of the museum, inquiries are still welcome at the postal address, telephone number or email address shown.

Opening Hours: Temporarily closed for major refurbishment. Re-opening expected Spring 2011.

Admission: Free

Facilities: Adjacent car parking, toilets, restaurant/café, shop, disabled access, lecture room

Warminster

INFANTRY AND SMALL ARMS SCHOOL CORPS
WEAPONS COLLECTION

HQ Small Arms School Corps, Land
Warfare Centre, Imber Road,
Warminster, Wiltshire BA12 0DJ
T: 01985 222487 / F: 01985 222211
E: regsecsasc@btconnect.com

Curator: Major Norman Benson

*A comprehensive collection of small arms tracing their
development from the 16th Century to the present day.*

Exhibits include pistols, sub-machine guns, rifles, light and
medium machine guns, light and medium mortars and anti-armour
weapons. The collection also contains a fine reference library of
specialist books and documents covering small arms trials from
1853 to 1939. The collection is very much for the specialist rather
than the casual visitor and is unsuitable for young children.
Visitors are escorted at all times.

Opening Hours: Tue and Thu 9am–4.30pm. Wed 9am–12.30pm
By appointment only

Admission: Free, but donations are encouraged

Facilities: Parking, toilets, disabled access and library

The South

THE SOUTH

17

27 Oxford

20

26

16

Aldershot

13 **14** **15** **18**

19

Winchester

21 **22** **23** **24** **25**

Southampton

Aldershot:	**13**	Aldershot Military Museum
	14	Army Medical Services
	15	Army Physical Training Corps
Andover:	**16**	Museum of Army Chaplaincy
Buckingham:	**17**	Buckinghamshire Military Museum Trust
Farham:	**18**	Royal Military Police Museum
Middle Wallop:	**19**	Museum of Army Flying
Reading:	**20**	REME Museum of Technology
Winchester:	**21**	Adjutant General's Corps
	22	Gurkha Museum
	23	Horsepower – King's Royal Hussars
	24	Royal Green Jackets (Rifles) Museum
	25	Royal Hampshire Regiment
Windsor:	**26**	Royal Berkshire Yeomanry Cavalry
Woodstock:	**27**	Soldiers of Oxfordshire Museum

Aldershot

ALDERSHOT MILITARY MUSEUM

Regular bus service from Aldershot or Farnborough town station to Queens Avenue; or turn off A325 to Aldershot Military Town and follow the signs

Aldershot Military Museum,
Queen's Avenue, Aldershot,
Hampshire GU11 2LG
T: 01252 314598 / F: 01252 342942
E: musmsa@hants.gov.uk
www.hants.gov.uk/museum/aldershot

Curator: Sally Day

The museum tells the story of the home of the British Army from 1854 to the present day, as well as the local history of Aldershot and Farnborough. From the Victorian Soldier to National Service, the museum uses photographs, models, displays and 'hands on' activities to give an insight into a soldier's domestic and military life. The local history gallery shows the growth and development of Aldershot Military Town and the birth of British aviation at Farnborough. Artillery guns and military vehicles are displayed in the grounds of the museum and the Montgomery Gallery.

Opening Hours: Daily 10am–5pm. Closed Christmas and New Year

Admission: Adults £2.50, Seniors £2, Children £1, Family ticket (2 adults + 2 children) £5, Groups £1.50 or £1, School parties £20 per hour – facilitated session.

Facilities: Parking, toilets, shop, disabled access, education service

ARMY MEDICAL SERVICES MUSEUM

Taxi from Farnborough or Ash Vale railway stations. By road from M3 exit 4 on A331 for 1.5 miles to exit for Mytchett then follow

brown signs for Army Medical Services Museum

Army Medical Services Museum, Keogh Barracks, Ash Vale, Aldershot, Hampshire GU12 5RQ
T: 01252 868612 / F: 01252 868832
E: armymedicalmuseum@btinternet.com
www.ams-museum.org.uk

Curator: Captain Pete Starling

Royal Army Medical Corps, Army Medical Department, Army Hospital Corps, Medical Staff Corps, Royal Army Veterinary Corps, Army Veterinary Corps, Veterinary Medical Department, Royal Army Dental Corps, Army Nursing Service, Territorial Army Nursing Service, Queen Alexandra's Royal Army Nursing Corps, Queen Alexandra's Imperial Military Nursing Service.

The museum covers the history of military medicine, veterinary science, nursing and dentistry from 1660 to the present. Included amongst the displays are uniforms, medals and insignia, medical and surgical instruments and military ambulances.

Opening Hours: Mon–Fri 10am–3.30pm. Weekends and evenings by appointement

Admission: Free

Facilities: Parking, toilets, shop, disabled access, children's activities

ARMY PHYSICAL TRAINING CORPS MUSEUM

By regular bus service from Aldershot, Farnborough and North Camp station, or via M3 using exits 4 and 4a and then A331

Army Physical Training Corps Museum,
Army School of PT, Fox Lines,
Queen's Avenue, Aldershot,
Hampshire GU11 2LB
T: 01252 347168
E: aptcmuseum@aspt.mod.uk
www.army.mod.uk/aptc

Curator: Major (Ret'd) RJ Kelly

Army Physical Training Corps, Army Physical Training Staff, Army Gymnastics Staff

The items and memorabilia on display tell the story of physical training in the Army from 1860 to the present day. Exhibits concentrate on the theme of the soldier-sportsman and there is an interesting display relating to members of the Corps who have represented their country at International and Olympic level. Access to the Corps archive may be obtained by appointment.

Opening Hours: Mon–Thu 9.30am–4.30pm, Fri 9.30am–12.30pm; Evenings and weekends by appointment

Admission: Free

Facilities: Parking, toilets, shop, disabled access, lecture room

Andover

MUSEUM OF ARMY CHAPLAINCY

 Museum of Army Chaplaincy, Armed Forces Chaplaincy Centre, Amport House, Andover, Hampshire SP11 8BG
T: 01264 773144 Ext 4248 / F: 01264 771042
E: museumcurator@amporthouse.co.uk
www.army.mod.uk/chaplains

Curator: David Blake

A unique display celebrating the work of army chaplains through the years including silver, uniforms, medals and documents.

Opening Hours: Mon–Fri 9am–5pm, appointments strongly recommended

Admission: Free

Facilities: Parking, toilets, shop, disabled access

Buckingham

BUCKINGHAMSHIRE MILITARY MUSEUM TRUST

 Buckinghamshire Military Museum Trust Collection, The Old Gaol Museum, Market Hill, Buckingham MK18 1JX
T: 01280.823020 / E: i.beckett@kent.ac.uk

Curator: Professor Ian FW Beckett

Royal Bucks King's Own Militia, Royal Buckinghamshire Hussars, Buckinghamshire Rifle Volunteers, Buckinghamshire Territorial Force and Territorial Army Battalions, Bucks Volunteer Training Corps, Buckinghamshire Home Guard.

A display of items associated with the auxiliary military forces of Buckinghamshire. The archives are housed separately in the Centre for Buckinghamshire Studies in Aylesbury, and there is a small subsidiary display in Claydon House (National Trust) near Winslow.

Opening Hours: Apr–Oct: Mon–Sat 10am–4pm. Sun 2pm–4pm.

Admission: Adults £1, Seniors/Children 50p. Groups and school parties by appointment

Facilities: Toilets, refreshments, shop, disabled access, lecture room

Fareham

ROYAL MILITARY POLICE MUSEUM

From railway station by 260 bus to museum on A286 Chichester-Midhurst road

 Royal Military Police Museum
Defence College of Policing, PPt 38, Southwick Park, Fareham, Hampshire PO17 6EJ
T: 023 9228 4372 / F: 023 9228 4406
E: museum_rhqrmp@btconnect.com
www.army.mod.uk/agc/provost/13312.aspx

Director: Lt Col (Retd) J.H. Baber
Curator: Richard Callaghan

Corps of Royal Military Police, Corps of Military Police, Military Foot Police, Military Mounted Police, Military Provost Staff Corps, Military Prison Staff Corps

The museum traces the history of military police from its origins to current operations in support of the UN and NATO. Artefacts range from Napoleonic medals to an illicit still from a Displaced Persons camp in Hamburg. Special displays include Close Protection, the role of the Special Investigation Branch and operations in Northern Ireland. A library and limited research facilities are available by prior arrangement. The Museum is located within the Defence Police College, therefore all visits are by arrangement. Also on site is the D-Day wall map, used by the Allied Supreme Command – this can be viewed by prior appointment. For news and information, please visit the museum website.

Opening Hours: Open by appointment. Please telephone in advance and bring photographic ID.

Admission: Free. Groups and school parties by arrangement

Facilities: Parking, toilets, shop

Middle Wallop

MUSEUM OF ARMY FLYING

Between Salisbury and Andover on the A343

 Museum of Army Flying, Middle Wallop, Stockbridge, Hampshire SO20 8DY
T: 01264 784421 / F: 01264 781694
E: administration@flying-museum.org.uk
www.flying-museum.org.uk

Director: Neil Martin

Army Aviation, Army Air Corps, Glider Pilot Regiment, Royal Artillery Air Observation Squadrons, Royal Flying Corps

Situated at Middle Wallop and adjacent to the Army Air Corps' busy working airfield, the Museum of Army Flying is packed with historic helicopters, aeroplanes, kites and gliders, dioramas, exhibits and displays, all telling the story of 'soldiers in the air' from late 19th-century balloons to the present day and attack helicopters. Plus simulators, 1940s house, rifle ranges, children's centre, gift shop, cinema, licensed café with airfield views, picnic area and plenty of free parking for coaches and cars.

Opening Hours: Daily 10am–4.30pm (except Christmas week)

Admission: Adults £7.50, Seniors/Students £5.50, Children (5–16 years) £5, Family ticket (2+2) £22. Groups by arrangement

Facilities: Parking, restaurant, toilets, lecture room, shop, disabled access, corporate facilities. Available for corporate and private hire.

Reading

REME MUSEUM OF TECHNOLOGY

By train to Reading/Wokingham, then by bus. By road, along A327 from Reading to Arborfield Garrison

 REME Museum of Technology,
Isaac Newton Road, Arborfield, Reading, Berkshire RG2 9NJ
T: 0118 9763375 / F: 0118 9762017
E: enquiries@rememuseum.org.uk
www.rememuseum.org.uk

Director: Lieutenant Colonel IW Cleasby

'REME exists to keep the punch in the Army's fist'
 – (Field Marshal The Viscount Montgomery of Alamein)

The Museum reflects the proud history and role of the Corps of the Royal Electrical and Mechanical Engineers. Spread over a four-and-a-half acre site, the Museum has a comprehensive collection of artefacts and exhibits illustrating the extensive scope of the REME Tradesman's responsibilities and activities in maintaining and repairing the Army's inventory of equipment. The spectacular displays include examples of wheeled, tracked and armoured recovery and repair vehicles, medals, pictures and one of the finest small arms collections in the country. The Museum is home to the Corps archives containing an extensive collection of documents, records, photographs and technical handbooks. A calendar of family events is published on the Museum's website (rememuseum.org.uk), and a comprehensive education service is available to schools.

Opening Hours: Mon–Thu 9am–4.30pm, Fri 9am–4pm, Sun 11am–4pm

Admission: Adults £5, Seniors £3.50, Children £4 (under 5s free), Family ticket £15 (2+3), Groups £4.40 for 10+. School parties by arrangement

Facilities: Parking, toilets, café, restaurant, shop, disabled access, lecture room, corporate hospitalities

Winchester

ADJUTANT GENERAL'S CORPS MUSEUM 21

At the upper end of the city centre, close to the Great Hall and Westgate

Adjutant General's Corps Museum Collection,
The Guardroom, Peninsula Barracks,
Romsey Road, Winchester,
Hampshire SO23 8TS
T: 01962 877826
E: curator@agcmuseum.co.uk

Curator: Ian Bailey

Adjutant General's Corps, Corps of Royal Military Police and Provost Staff Corps, Royal Army Pay Corps, Army Pay Corps, Army Pay Department, Royal Army Education Corps, Army Education Corps, Corps of Army Schoolmasters, Women's Royal Army Corps, Auxiliary Territorial Service, Women's Army Auxiliary Corps, Army Legal Corps, Army Legal Staff

The Adjutant General's Corps was formed in 1992 and the museum tells the histories of those corps from which it was formed using text, images, objects, uniforms and realistic figure reconstructions.

Opening Hours: Tue–Sat 10am–5pm,
Bank Holidays 12pm–4pm. Closed Sundays

Admission: Free

Facilities: Parking (by arrangement), toilets, café

THE GURKHA MUSEUM 22

At the upper end of the city centre, close to the Great Hall and Westgate

Gurkha Museum, Peninsula Barracks, Romsey Road, Winchester, Hampshire SO23 8TS
T: 01962 842832/843659
F: 01962 877597
E: curator@thegurkhamuseum.co.uk
www.thegurkhamuseum.co.uk

Curator: Major Gerald Davies

Royal Gurkha Rifles, 1st King George V's Own Gurkha Rifles (The Malaun Regiment), 2nd King Edward VII's Own Gurkha Rifles (The Sirmoor Rifles), 3rd Queen Alexandra's Own Gurkha Rifles, 4th Prince of Wales's Own Gurkha Rifles, 5th Royal Gurkha Rifles (Frontier Force), 6th Queen Elizabeth's Own Gurkha Rifles, 7th Duke Of Edinburgh's Own Gurkha Rifles, 8th Gurkha Rifles, 9th Gurkha Rifles, 10th Princess Mary's Own Gurkha Rifles, 11th Gurkha Rifles (1918–22), Queen's Gurkha Engineers, Queen's Gurkha Signals, Queen's Own Gurkha Transport Regiment, Western or Bettiah Corps (1813–26), Eastern or Rungpore Battalion (1815–30), 2nd Nusseri Battalion (1815–16), Gorakhpore Hill Rangers (1815–16), Sylhet Frontier Corps (1817–23), 4th Regiment of Infantry, Shah Shooja's Force (1840–3), 2nd Assam Sebundy Corps (1839–44), Nusseree Battalion (1850–61), 7th Gurkha Rifles (1902–07), 153 (Gurkha) Parachute Battalion (1941–7), 154 (Gurkha) Parachute Battalion (1943–6), 5th/3rd Gurkha Rifles (1942), 25th Gurkha Rifles (1942–6), 26th Gurkha Rifles (1943–6), 14th Gurkha Rifles (1943–6), 29th Gurkha Rifles (1943–6), 38th Gurkha Rifles (1943–6), 56th Gurkha Rifles (1943–6), 710th Gurkha Rifles (1943–6), Boys Company (1948–68), Gurkha Military Police (1949–70), Staff Band Brigade of Gurkhas, Gurkha Independent Parachute Company (1961–71), Assam Rifles, Burma Military Police (1886–1948), Burma Frontier Force (1886–1948), Burma Regiment (1886–1948), Burma Rifles (1915–42), Jammu and Kashmir Units, 11th Gorkha Rifles

The Gurkha Museum tells the story of Gurkha service to the Crown since 1815, covering the Indian Mutiny, North-West Frontier, both World Wars, post-Empire conflicts in Vietnam, Indonesia, Hong Kong, and the Falkland Islands and a variety of more recent UN operations including Zaire, the Gulf, Bosnia, Kosovo, East Timor, Sierra Leone, Iraq and Afghanistan. The collection also reflects the art and culture of Nepal. There is also an extensive library and archive facility available by prior appointment.

Opening Hours: Mon–Sat 10am–5pm, Sun 12pm–4pm

Admission: Adults £2, Seniors £1, Children and Servicemen free. Groups and school parties by arrangement

Facilities: Parking, toilets, lecture room, shop, disabled access, corporate events

THE SOUTH

HORSEPOWER – THE MUSEUM OF THE KING'S ROYAL HUSSARS 23

At the upper end of the city centre, close to the Great Hall and Westgate

The King's Royal Hussars Museum,
Peninsula Barracks, Romsey Road,
Winchester, Hampshire SO23 8TS
T: 01962 828539 / F: 01962 828538
E: curator@horsepowermuseum.co.uk
www.horsepowermuseum.co.uk

Curator: Major Robin Boon

The King's Royal Hussars, The Royal Hussars (Prince of Wales's Own), 10th Royal Hussars (Prince of Wales's Own), 10th (Prince of Wales's Own Royal) Hussars, 10th (Prince of Wales's Own) Hussars, 10th (Prince of Wales's Own) Light Dragoons, 10th Dragoons, 11th Hussars (Prince Albert's Own), 11th (Prince Albert's Own) Hussars, 11th Light Dragoons, 11th Dragoons, Gore's Dragoons, Churchill's Dragoons, Cobham's Dragoons, Honeywood's Dragoons, Kerr's Dragoons

A comprehensive collection of uniforms, medals, weapons, paintings, photographs, regimental silver and guidons trace the history of The King's Royal Hussars and its predecessor regiments from their foundation in 1715 to the present day. The museum has recently re-opened after extensive refurbishment. Access to the archives is available by prior appointment.

Opening Hours: Tue–Fri 10am–12.45pm and 1.15pm–4pm. Sat, Sun and holidays 12pm–4pm

Admission: Free. Groups and school parties by appoinment

Facilities: Parking, toilets, shop, disabled access

ROYAL GREEN JACKETS (RIFLES) MUSEUM 24

At the upper end of the city centre, close to the Great Hall and Westgate

Royal Green Jackets (Rifles) Museum,
Peninsula Barracks,
Romsey Road, Winchester,
Hampshire SO23 8TS
T: 01962 828549 / F: 01962 828534
E: curator@rgjmuseum.co.uk
www.rgjmuseum.co.uk

Curator: Christine Pullen

The Rifles, Royal Green Jackets, 1st Green Jackets, Oxfordshire and Buckinghamshire Light Infantry, 43rd (Monmouthshire Light Infantry) Regiment of Foot, 43rd (or the Monmouthshire) Regiment of Foot (Light Infantry), 43rd (or the Monmouthshire) Regiment of Foot, 43rd Regiment of Foot, Colonel Fowke's Regiment of Foot, 54th Foot (re-numbered 43rd Foot), 52nd (Oxfordshire Light Infantry) Regiment, 52nd (Oxfordshire) Regiment of Foot, Colonel Lambton's Regiment of Foot, 54th Foot (re-numbered 52nd Foot), 2nd Green Jackets (King's Royal Rifle Corps), King's Royal Rifle Corps, 60th or The King's Royal Rifle Corps Regiment of Foot, 60th or The Duke of York's Own Rifle Corps, 60th (Royal American) Regiment of Foot, 62nd or The Royal American Regiment of Foot (re-numbered 60th Foot), 3rd Green Jackets (Rifle Brigade), Rifle Brigade (Prince Consort's Own), Rifle Brigade (The Prince Consort's Own), Prince Consort's Own Rifle Brigade, Rifle Brigade, 95th Rifle Regiment, 1800 Experimental Corps of Riflemen or Rifle Corps

An outstanding collection of uniforms, weapons, silver, paintings and medals, including 34 of the Regiment's 59 Victoria Crosses, all impressively displayed, record the history of the Royal Green Jackets and its antecedent regiments from 1741 to the present day. Amongst several models is a magnificent diorama of Waterloo with 22,000 model soldiers and horses and an accompanying sound and light commentary. The regimental archive is housed in a separate building on site and may be viewed by appointment.

Opening Hours: Mon–Sat 10am–5pm. Sunday closed.

Admission: Adult £3, Seniors £2, Children/Students £1.50, Family ticket £6. Groups and school parties by appointment only

Facilities: Toilets, shop, disabled access. Parking nearby

ROYAL HAMPSHIRE REGIMENT MUSEUM **25**

Just off the city centre, near the Great Hall and other regimental museums

 Royal Hampshire Regiment Museum,
Serle's House, Southgate Street,
Winchester, Hampshire SO23 9EG
T: 01962 863658 / F: 01962 888302
E: museum@serlehouse.co.uk
www.royalhampshireregimentmuseum.co.uk

Princess of Wales's Royal Regiment (Queen's and Royal Hampshires), Royal Hampshire Regiment, Hampshire Regiment, 37th (or the North Hampshire) Regiment of Foot, 37th Regiment of Foot, Gray's Regiment of Foot, Stuart's Regiment of Foot, de Jean's Regiment of Foot, Munro's Regiment of Foot, Ponsonby's Regiment of Foot, Murray's Regiment of Foot, Hinchinbroke's Regiment of Foot, Fane's Regiment of Foot, Windress's Regiment of Foot, Meredith's Regiment of Foot, 67th (or South Hampshire) Regiment of Foot, 67th Regiment of Foot, 2nd Battalion 20th Foot, 67th (South Hampshire) Regiment of Foot, 6th (Duke of Connaught's Own) Battalion The Hampshire Regiment, 8th (Princess Beatrice's Own Isle of Wight Rifles) Battalion The Hampshire Regiment, 11th (Royal Militia of Jersey) Battalion The Hampshire Regiment.

The collection of Hampshire's County Regiment, the Militia, Rifle Volunteers and Volunteers from 1702 onwards. The Museum is located in the extremely handsome Serle's House *c.*1730, former headquarters of The Royal Hampshire Regiment. The regimental archive is held in the same building and may be viewed by appointment. The Memorial Garden is dedicated to all those members of the Regiment who have died in the service of their country.

Opening Hours: Mon–Fri 10am–4pm
Apr–Oct: weekends and Bank Holidays 12pm–4pm

Admission: Free

Facilities: Parking, toilets, shop, lecture room

Windsor

ROYAL BERKSHIRE YEOMANRY CAVALRY MUSEUM **26**

At the junction of Wood Street and Bolton Street. From town centre follow signs to the Great Park and turn right into Bolton Street at the 40mph sign

 Royal Berkshire Yeomanry Cavalry Museum, TA Centre, Bolton Road,
Windsor, Berkshire SL4 3JG
T: 01753 860600 / F: 01753 854946
E: andrewfrench@hotmail.com
www.army.mod.uk/signals/
organisation/8748.aspx?rating

Curator: Brigadier AP Verey and Captain AG French

The museum contains a well-displayed and comprehensive collection tracing the history of the Regiment since its beginnings in 1794.

Opening Hours: Tue 7.30pm–9.30pm by appointment only

Admission: Free

Facilities: Toilets, limited disabled access. Parking nearby

THE SOUTH

Woodstock

SOLDIERS OF OXFORDSHIRE MUSEUM `27`

Off the A44 at Woodstock, 5 miles north of Oxford

Soldiers of Oxfordshire Museum
The Old Tannery, Hensington Road,
Woodstock OX20 1JL
T: 01993 813 832
E: secretary@sofo.org.uk
www.sofo.org.uk

The **SOFO Project Manager** is Major Hugh
Babington Smith, to whom all inquiries
should be addressed, by email to
research@sofo.org.uk or by telephone to
01993 813 832 (answerphone)

*Royal Green Jackets, Oxfordshire & Buckinghamshire Light
Infantry, 43rd (Monmouthshire Light Infantry) Regiment of Foot,
43rd (or the Monmouthshire) Regiment of Foot (Light Infantry),
43RD (or The Monmouthshire) Regiment of Foot, Colonel Fowke's
Regiment of Foot, 54th Foot (re-numbered 43rd of Foot), 52nd
(Oxfordshire Light Infantry) Regiment, 52nd (Oxfordshire)
Regiment of Foot, 52nd Regiment of Foot, 54th (Oxfordshire)
Regiment of Foot (re-numbered 52nd of Foot). The Queen's Own
Oxfordshire Hussar, Oxfordshire University OTC, Home Guard.*

The Soldiers of Oxfordshire is a new venture representing the
County regiments of Oxfordshire. Principal amongst these is the
Oxfordshire and Buckinghamshire Light Infantry, which has a small
but comprehensive collection of uniforms, weapons and other
artefacts covering the period from its formation in 1741 to its
amalgamation into the Royal Green Jackets in 1966. The collection
is now owned by the Royal Green Jackets Museum Trust.

The museum also houses the regimental collection of The Queen's
Own Oxfordshire Hussars, with militaria and archives covering the
history of the Regiment from its formation in about 1794 to the
present day, through its different roles as Yeomanry, Artillery and
Royal Signals. The collection is owned by the Oxfordshire
Yeomanry Trust.

The majority of the collections are in storage pending re-location
to new premises under the auspices of the Soldiers of Oxfordshire
Trust (SOFO). Opening is anticipated in 2012. The Trust has
retained a small number of objects and the medal collection for
display at the above address where visitors and researchers are
welcome by appointment. The Trust also has an exhibition at the
Oxfordshire Museum in Woodstock (www.oxfordshire.gov.uk/
theoxfordshiremuseum).

South East

LONDON

34

28 **29**

36

35

33

30

Southampton

Brighton

37 **31** **32**

Camberley:	**28**	Royal Logistic Corps
	29	Royal Military Academy Sandhurst
Canterbury:		The Buffs, Royal East Kent Regiment Museum Collection *See p30* **38**
Dover:	**30**	Princess of Wales's Royal Regiment and The Queen's Regiment
Eastbourne:	**31**	Queen's Royal Irish Hussars
	32	Royal Sussex Regiment
Edenbridge:	**33**	Kent and Sharpshooters Yeomanry
Gillingham:	**34**	Royal Engineers
Guildford:	**35**	Queen's Royal Surrey Regiment
Maidstone:	**36**	Queen's Own Royal West Kent Regiment
Newhaven:	**37**	Sussex and Surrey Yeomanry

Camberley

ROYAL LOGISTIC CORPS MUSEUM 28

Bus no 48 from Brookwood railway station, bus no 35 from Woking or by car via M3 (Junct 3) and along B3015

 Royal Logistic Corps Museum, Princess Royal Barracks, Deepcut, Camberley, Surrey GU16 6RW
T: 01252 833371 / F: 01252 833484
E: information@rlcmuseum.com
www.army.mod.uk/rlc

Director: Andrew Robertshaw

Royal Logistic Corps, Royal Corps of Transport, Royal Army Service Corps, Army Service Corps, Commissariat and Transport Corps, Commissariat and Transport Department, Control Department, Commissariat Department, Military Train, Land Transport Corps, Royal Waggon Train, Corps of Waggoners, Royal Army Ordnance Corps, Army Ordnance Corps, Army Ordnance Department, Ordnance Store Corps, Ordnance Store Department, Ordnance Store Branch, Control Department, Military Store Staff Corps, Military Stores Department, Corps of Armourer-Sergeants, Royal Pioneer Corps, Pioneer Corps, Auxiliary Military Pioneer Corps, Labour Corps, Army Catering Corps, Royal Engineers Postal and Courier Service

The museum, recently modernised and refurbished, houses a comprehensive collection relating to the history and activities of the Royal Logistic Corps and its several antecedent corps. Displays include uniforms, medals, weapons and historical artefacts portraying the development of military logistics from the Middle Ages to the present day. Access to the extensive Corps archive is available by appointment.

Opening Hours: Mon–Fri 9am–4pm, Sat 12pm–4pm 31 Mar to 1 Oct only. Closed Sunday, Bank Holidays and Christmas Eve to New Year

Admission: Free. Groups and school parties by appointment

Facilities: Parking, toilets, shop, disabled access

ROYAL MILITARY ACADEMY SANDHURST 29

Train to Camberley or London-Fareham coach to Cambridge Hotel. Main entrance on A30

 Royal Military Academy Sandhurst Collection, Camberley, Surrey GU15 4PQ
T: 01276 412489/2483 / F: 01276 412595
Research enquiries to:
dr.morton@rmas.mod.uk

Curator: Dr Anthony Morton
Deputy: Sebastian Puncher

Royal Military Academy Sandhurst, Royal Military Academy Woolwich, Royal Military College Sandhurst

The small museum contains displays of uniforms, paintings, photographs and other artefacts relating to the history of the Royal Military Academy, Woolwich, The Royal Military College, Sandhurst and the Royal Military Academy Sandhurst. The collection also embraces the Academy's historic archive including the gentlemen cadet registers.

Opening Hours: By appointment only

Facilities: Parking, toilets, lecture room

Canterbury

THE BUFFS, ROYAL EAST KENT REGIMENT MUSEUM COLLECTION

See p30 38

SOUTH EAST

Dover

PRINCESS OF WALES'S ROYAL REGIMENT AND QUEEN'S REGIMENT MUSEUM

Access by car, minibus or taxi from town centre

 Princess of Wales's Royal Regiment and Queen's Regiment Museum, 5 Keep Yard, Dover Castle, Dover, Kent CT16 1HU
T: 01304 240121 / F: 01304 240121
E: pwrrqueensmuseum@tinyworld.co.uk
www.army.mod.uk/pwrr

Curator: Major A Martin, RHQ, PWRR, Howe Barracks, Canterbury CT1 1JY
T: 01227 818053 / F: 01227 818057
E: rhq@123pwrr.co.uk

Princess of Wales's Royal Regiment (Queen's and Royal Hampshires), Queen's Regiment, 1st Bn Queen's Regiment (Queen's Surrey), 2nd Bn Queen's Regiment (Queen's Own Buffs), 3rd Bn Queen's Regiment (Royal Sussex), 4th Bn Queen's Regiment (Middlesex)

The collection traces the history of the Princess of Wales's Royal Regiment – direct successor of twelve forebear regiments – through four-and-a-quarter centuries of service to the Crown. Starting in 1572 with the deployment of a Tudor company to support the Dutch in their war against the Spanish, moving on to the raising of a regiment in 1661 to garrison the North African port of Tangier, which earned the first ever awarded battle honour 'Tangier 1662–80'. A series of displays, interactive videos and recordings takes the visitor right up to the Regiment's most recent operations in support of the UN and NATO.

Opening Hours: Apr–Sep: 10am–6pm. Oct: 10am–5pm. Nov–Mar: 10am–4pm

Admission: Free with Castle entry. Groups and school parties by appointment. For details of Castle entry fee contact English Heritage Dover Castle at Tel 01304 211067 or www.english-heritage.org.uk

Facilities: Parking, toilets, refreshments, shop, lecture room

Eastbourne

QUEEN'S ROYAL IRISH HUSSARS MUSEUM

The Redoubt is ½ a mile east of Eastbourne Pier and 1 mile from Eastbourne Bus Station. Buses 1, 2, 5, 10 and 11 stop nearby on Seaside and Bus 99 stops on Royal Parade

 Queen's Royal Irish Hussars Museum, Part of the Queen's Royal Hussars Collection, Redoubt Fortress, Eastbourne, East Sussex BN22 7AQ
T: 01323 410300 / F: 01323 438827
E: redoubtmuseum@eastbourne.gov.uk
www.eastbournemuseums.co.uk

Curator: Jo Seaman (Museum Officer)

Queen's Royal Irish Hussars, 8th King's Royal Irish Hussars, 8th Light Dragoons, Cunningham's Dragoons, 4th Queen's Own Hussars, 4th Light Dragoons

An important collection covering this distinguished Regiment's history from its formation in 1693 to the Gulf War. Displays include items from the Charge of the Light Brigade and a fine collection of medals. The collection is displayed within the Redoubt Fortress. This circular Napoleonic fort is one of the best preserved in the country. Built between 1804 and 1810 at a time when Napoleon was threatening to invade England it forms, along with 74 Martello towers, a string of coastal defences stretching from Folkestone to Seaford. Originally housing anything up to 250 soldiers, the Redoubt provides the perfect setting for this regimental collection. Alongside the collections of The Queen's Royal Irish Hussars and the Sussex Combined Services, it forms the largest military museum in the south.

Opening Hours: Apr–Nov: Tues–Sun 10am–5pm
Closed Mondays except Bank Holidays

Admission: Adults £4, Seniors/Students £3, Children £2, Family ticket £8 (2+2), School parties £1.50 per child

Facilities: Toilets, café, shop

SOUTH EAST

ROYAL SUSSEX REGIMENT 32

On the seafront 0.5 miles east of the pier. A 20-minute walk from the station or Nos 1, 2, 3, 9, 22 buses from the town centre stop nearby on Seaside Road

Royal Sussex Regimental Collection, Redoubt, Royal Parade Eastbourne, East Sussex BN22 7AQ
T: 01323 410300 / F: 01323 438827
E: redoubtmuseum@.gov.uk
www.eastbournemuseums.co.uk

Curator: Jo Seaman (Museum Officer)

Royal Sussex Regiment, 35th (Royal Sussex) Regiment, 35th (or The Sussex) Regiment of Foot, 35th (or The Dorsetshire) Regiment of Foot, 35th Regiment of Foot, Earl of Donegal's Regiment of Foot – The Belfast Regiment, 107th Bengal Infantry Regiment, 3rd (Bengal Light Infantry) Regiment, 3rd (Bengal European Light Infantry) Regiment (Honourable East India Company)

The collection of the County Regiment of Sussex covering its history from the raising of its antecedent regiments in 1701 under the 3rd Earl of Donegall, to its amalgamation into The Queen's Regiment in 1966. Collection highlights include a display of rare headdress badges, and impressive collections of uniforms and medals, as well as a German staff car captured in the desert in 1943.

The collection is displayed within the Redoubt Fortress. This circular Napoleonic fort is one of the best preserved in the country. Built between 1804-10 at a time when Napoleon was threatening to invade England it forms, along with 74 Martello towers, a string of coastal defences stretching from Folkestone to Seaford. Originally housing anything up to 250 soldiers the Redoubt provides the perfect setting for this regimental collection. Alongside the collections of The Queen's Royal Irish Hussars and the Sussex Combined Services, it forms the largest military museum in the south.

Opening Hours: 15 Apr–12 Nov: Tue–Sun 10am–5.00pm. Closed Mon except Bank Holidays. Otherwise by appointment

Admission: Adults £4, Seniors/Students £3, Children £2, Family ticket £8 (2+2), School parties £1.50 per child.

Facilities: Toilets, shop

Edenbridge

KENT AND SHARPSHOOTERS YEOMANRY MUSEUM 33

Off B2027 Edenbridge-Marlpit Hill Road. Rail, Hever station, 1 mile (no taxis). Taxi from Edenbridge town, 3 miles away

Kent and Sharpshooters Yeomanry Museum, Hever Castle, Edenbridge, Kent TN8 7NG
T: 01732 865224
E: ksymuseum@aol.com
www.ksymuseum.org.uk

Curator: Major Boris Mollo

Royal East Kent Mounted Rifles, Queen's Own West Kent Yeomanry, The Kent Yeomanry, 3rd County of London Yeomanry (Sharpshooters), 23rd London Armoured Company (Sharpshooters), 4th County of London Yeomanry (Sharpshooters), 3rd/4th County of London Yeomanry (Sharpshooters), Kent and County of London Yeomanry (Sharpshooters), Kent and Sharpshooters Yeomanry

Uniforms, medals, badges, pictures and photographs reflecting the history of the Regiment and its predecessors. A further display and the regimental archive may be seen by appointment at Sharpshooters House, Mitcham Road, Croydon, Surrey CR0 3RU. Tel: 020 8688 2138.

Opening Hours: 1 Mar–31 Oct: 12pm–6pm daily. Last admissions at 5pm. Limited opening Nov–Mar, check times with Castle.

Admission: Included in Castle entry fees – Adults £13, Seniors £11, Children £7, Family ticket £33 (2+2). Groups by appointment.

Facilities: Parking, toilets, refreshments, shop, disabled access

SOUTH EAST

Gillingham

ROYAL ENGINEERS MUSEUM

Taxi or 1-mile walk from Gillingham station. By road from Gillingham: A231 from town centre towards Chatham, turn right at traffic lights into Prince Arthur Road. From Chatham: A231 from town centre towards Gillingham, left at roundabout into Wood Street and left at traffic lights into Prince Arthur Road

Royal Engineers Museum,
Brompton Barracks, Prince Arthur Road, Gillingham, Kent ME4 4UG
T: 01634 822839 / F: 01634 822371
E: mail@re-museum.co.uk
www.remuseum.org.uk

Curator: Rebecca Nash

Corps of Royal Engineers, Royal Engineers, Corps of Royal Sappers and Miners, Corps of Royal Military Artificers, Indian Engineers including Bengal, Bombay and Madras groups, East India Company Engineer Groups, Royal Engineers Submarine Service, Royal Engineers Bomb Disposal, Military Survey

The Royal Engineers Museum and Library tell the story of the Corps of Royal Engineers and military engineering. It is a story about the Sappers and their courage, creativity and innovation. In peace and war the Corps has been everywhere and involved in everything. The museum galleries display exquisite Chinese embroideries given to General Gordon, drawings, letters and airgraphs, paintings and fine uniforms alongside Zulu shields from Rorke's Drift, tanks, torpedoes, bridges and chemical weapons. The Library, founded in 1813, holds material as diverse as 1860s photographs of Canada, classic military histories and World War I unit war diaries.

Opening Hours: Tue–Fri 9am–5pm, Sat/Sun/Bank Holidays 11.30am–5pm. Closed Mon, Christmas week and New Year's Day

Admission: Adults £7.13, Seniors/Students/Children £4.75, Children under 5 Free, Family ticket (2+2) £19. Groups and school parties – prices on application.

Facilities: Parking, toilets, shop, disabled access, lecture room

Guildford

QUEEN'S ROYAL SURREY REGIMENT MUSEUM

The museum stands 300 yards north of the A246 and A247 junction. From Clandon station, Guildford-Leatherhead bus to Clandon crossroads

Queen's Royal Surrey Regiment Museum,
Clandon Park, Guildford, Surrey GU4 7RQ
T: 01483 223419 / F: 01483 223419
E: qrsregimentalmuseum@btconnect.com
www.queensroyalsurreys.org.uk

Curator: Ian Chatfield

Princess of Wales's Royal Regiment (Queen's and Royal Hampshires), Queen's Royal Surrey Regiment, Queen's Royal Regiment (West Surrey), Queen's (Royal West Surrey) Regiment, Royal West Surrey Regiment (The Queen's), Royal West Surreys, Princess of Wales's Own Regiment of Foot, Queen's Royal Regiment, Queen's (Second) Royal Regiment of Foot, Queen's Own Royal Regiment of Foot, Queen Dowager's Regiment of Foot, Queen Dowager's Regiment, Queen's Regiment, Henry Mordaunt, Earl of Peterborough – The Tangier Regiment, East Surrey Regiment, 31st (Huntingdonshire) Regiment, 31st (or Huntingdonshire) Regiment of Foot, 31st Regiment of Foot, Villier's Regiment of Marines, Goring's Marines, Churchill's Marines, Luttrell's Marines, 70th (Surrey) Regiment, 70th (or The Glasgow Lowland) Regiment of Foot, Glasgow Greys, 70th (or The Surrey) Regiment of Foot, 70th Regiment of Foot

The museum re-opened recently after an extensive refurbishment. Housed in the National Trust property of Clandon Park, the museum tells the story of England's senior infantry regiment and its antecedent three County Regiments of Surrey in a comprehensive display of important objects covering the period 1661 to the present day. Researchers are welcome but are advised to contact the curator for an appointment.

Opening Hours: Easter to end Oct daily (less Mon, Fri and Sat) 12pm–5pm and Bank Holiday Mon.

Admission: Free, donations welcome

Facilities: Parking, toilets, refreshments, shop, disabled access

Maidstone

QUEEN'S OWN ROYAL WEST KENT REGIMENT COLLECTION 36

By road from London leave M20 at J6, from Folkestone leave M20 at J8 then join A20. Trains to Maidstone East station

 Queen's Own Royal West Kent Regiment Museum Collection, Maidstone Museum and Art Gallery, St Faith's Street, Maidstone, Kent ME4 1LH
T: 01622 602838 / F: 01622 685022
E: qorwkmuseum@maidstone.gov.uk
www.museum.maidstone.gov.uk/queensown

Curator: Giles Guthrie,
Keeper of Human History

Queen's Own Royal West Kent Regiment, Royal West Kent Regiment (Queen's Own), Queen's Own (Royal West Kent Regiment), 50th (Queen's Own) Regiment, 50th or The Queen's Regiment of Foot, 50th (or the Duke of Clarence's) Regiment of Foot, 50th (or West Kent) Regiment of Foot, 50th Regiment of Foot, 52nd Regiment of Foot, 97th (Earl of Ulster's) Regiment of Foot, 97th Regiment of Foot, 20th London Regiment, Deptford Volunteers, Loyal Greenwich Water Fencibles, Loyal Greenwich Volunteer Infantry, 3rd Kent Rifle Volunteers. 2nd Volunteer Bn The Queen's Own (Royal West Kent Regiment), 20th (County of London) Bn The London Regiment, 20th London Regiment (The Queen's Own), 34th (The Queen's Own, Royal West Kent) Anti Aircraft Battalion Royal Engineers, 34th (The Queen's Own, Royal West Kent) Searchlight Regiment Royal Artillery TA, 569 Searchlight Regiment RA (QORWK) TA, 569 (The Queen's Own)(M) LAA/SL Regiment RA TA, Q (The Queen's Own) Battery 265 LAA Regiment RA TA, 6th (Cyclist) Battalion The Queen's Own Royal West Kent Regiment, Kent Cyclists Battalion

A comprehensive regimental collection of uniforms, weapons, medals, pictures and campaign relics. It includes the personal effects of a number of distinguished soldiers such as Field Marshal Viscount Hardinge and General Sir Charles Napier.

Opening Hours: Mon–Fri 10am–5.15pm, Sun 11am–4pm

Admission: Free

Facilities: Toilets, refreshments, shop, disabled access

Newhaven

SUSSEX AND SURREY YEOMANRY COLLECTION 37

On A259 coast road. 1 mile from town centre

 Sussex and Surrey Yeomanry Museum Collection, Newhaven Fort, Newhaven, East Sussex BN9 9DL
T: 01273 517622
E: info@newhavenfort.org.uk
www.newhavenfort.org.uk

 Curator: Keith Fuller
T: 01273 611055 E: founded1794@aol.com

Opening Hours: 1 Mar–31 Oct: 10.30am–6pm daily (5pm in Oct)

Admission: Adults £5.95, Seniors £4.80, Children £3.90, Family ticket £18.50 (2+2/3). Groups and school parties by appointment.

Group visit rates: Adults £4.75, Concessions £3.85, Children £2.85, Schools £2.20.

Season tickets: Adult £17, Concessions £13.50, Children £11, Family ticket £47.50.

Facilities: Coach parking (by appt), toilets, café
Phone in advance to arrange disabled drop-off point and access

The Royal Scots Dragoon Guards Museum, Edinburgh Castle

123

During the Battle of Waterloo Ensign Kennedy was carrying the Battalion's King's Colour. When he was mortally wounded a Sergeant leapt forward to retrieve the Colour. Unable to release the Colour from Kennedy's grip he hoisted the officer over his shoulder and returned both Ensign and Colour to safety. It is worth noting that when the French saw this action unfolding they were so impressed that they held their fire until the rescue had been completed.

Guards Museum, London 40
Display of ceremonial uniforms

Durham Light Infantry Museum, Durham 113
A small section of the impressive medals collection

Museum of Army Flying, Middle Wallop 19
Lynx helicopter XX153 – 1972 holder of the helicopter world speed record at 321.74 kph

Enniskillen Castle in County Fermanagh
Home of the Royal Inniskilling Fusiliers Museum

Royal Inniskilling Fusiliers Museum, Enniskillen
A World War 2 group

Top: **The Wardrobe, Salisbury**   9
Museum of The Rifles (Berkshire & Wiltshire) and AMOT headquarters in Salisbury

Above: **Airborne Assault Museum, Duxford**   55
A display of equipment used by the Parachute Regiment and other Airborne Forces

Top right: **Royal Logistic Corps Museum, Deepcut**   28
Field Marshal Montgomery's Rolls Royce staff car

The Fusilier Museum, Bury
A mannequin in the uniform of the 20th Foot in the recently opened museum of the Royal Regiment of Fusiliers

91

Royal Anglian Regiment
Equipment and weaponry in a cold war display

The Tank Museum, Bovington
An early World War I tank

4

Shropshire Regimental Museum, Shewsbury
The regimental museum of the King's Shropshire Light Infantry

74

Firepower! Royal Artillery Museum, Woolwich
A selection of the firepower on display in the museum's Gunnery Hall

London

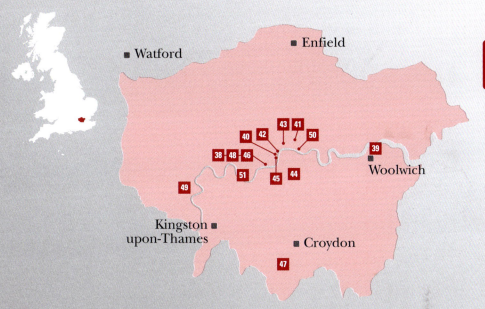

THE BUFFS, ROYAL EAST KENT REGIMENT MUSEUM COLLECTION

For directions, see entry for National Army Museum, London, p46

The Buffs, Royal East Kent Regiment Museum Collection
National Army Museum
Royal Hospital Road, London SW3 4HT
T: 0207 730 0717
E: a.massie@national-army-museum.ac.uk

Head of Archives: Dr Alastair Massie

Princess of Wales's Royal Regiment (Queen's and Royal Hampshires), Queen's Own Buffs, Royal Kent Regiment, Buffs (Royal East Kent Regiment), Buffs (East Kent Regiment), 3rd (East Kent, The Buffs) Regiment, 3rd (or the East Kent) Regiment of Foot, 3rd (or The Buffs) Regiment of Foot, Prince George of Denmark's Regiment of Foot, East Kent Volunteers and Militia

Ownership of the regimental collection of The Buffs has passed from Canterbury City Council to the National Army Museum, where the collection is now housed. It is planned to return a representative display to Canterbury's Beaney Institute when it re-opens in 2012.

A collection reflecting the history of one of England's oldest infantry regiments is now incorporated within the National Army Museum. The impressive array of pictures, medals, uniforms, mess silver and other artefacts traces the worldwide history of the Regiment from its formation in Elizabethan days to its amalgamation in 1961. The collection includes some items from the East Kent Volunteers and Militia. All research enquiries should be addressed to Dr Alastair Massie, Head of Archives, Photographs, Film and Sound at the National Army Museum.

For opening hours and other details: see National Army Museum entry on page 46.

FIREPOWER! THE ROYAL ARTILLERY MUSEUM

Nearest railway station, Woolwich Arsenal. Nearest Underground station, North Woolwich. Bus routes 472, 161, 96, 180 stop in Plumstead Road outside the Royal Arsenal. Bus routes 53, 54, 422, 380 stop in Woolwich town centre

Firepower! The Royal Artillery Museum,
Royal Arsenal, Woolwich, London SE18 6ST
T: 020 8855 7755 / F: 020 8855 7100
E: info@firepower.org.uk
www.firepower.org.uk

Curator: Mark Smith

Royal Regiment of Artillery, Royal Artillery, Royal Horse Artillery, Royal Field Artillery, Royal Garrison Artillery, Royal Irish Artillery, Artillery of the Honourable East India Company

Located at Woolwich, the historic home of the Regiment since 1716, the museum traces the Regiment's history from that time with a comprehensive display of artillery weapons in a collection of international standing. Alongside the uniforms, guns, medals, badges and other regimental memorabilia are exhibits that enable visitors to feel what it was like to be a 20th-century gunner in the ground-shaking field of fire, as the men and women who served in the Royal Artillery tell of their experiences. The science and technology of gunnery is explained with the help of hands-on interactive displays.

Opening Hours: Apr–Oct: Wed–Sun 10.30am–5pm. Nov–Mar: Fri, Sat, Sun 10.30am–5pm

Admission: Adults £5, Seniors £4.50, Children £2.50, Family ticket £12. Groups and school parties by arrangement

Facilities: Parking, toilets, restaurant, shop, disabled access, lecture room, corporate events

GUARDS MUSEUM

Nearest Underground, St James's Park. Access is from Birdcage Walk

Guards Museum, Wellington Barracks, Birdcage Walk, London SW1E 6HQ
T: 020 7414 3428 / F: 020 7414 3429
E: Guardsmuseum@aol.com
www.theguardsmuseum.com

Curator: Andrew Wallis

Grenadier Guards, 1st or Grenadier Regiment of Foot Guards, 1st Regiment of Foot Guards, King's Royal Regiment of Guards, His Majestie's Regiment of Guards (Wentworth's Regiment), Coldstream Guards, Coldstream Regiment of Foot Guards, Lord General's Regiment of Foot Guards, Lord General's Regiment of Foot, General Monck's Regiment (The Coldstreamers), Scots Guards, Scots Fusilier Guards, 3rd Regiment of Foot Guards, Scotch Guards (or Scotts Guards), The King's Lyfe Guards of Foot, The King's Foot Guards, The King's Regiment, His Majestie's Regiment of Guards, Our Regiment of Guards, New Regiment of Foot Guards, Argyll's Regiment of Royal Scotsmen, Irish Guards, Welsh Guards, Guards Camel Regiment, Machine Gun Guards, Guards Machine Gun Regiment, Guards Parachute Company

Uniforms, colours, weapons, silver, medals, pictures and many interesting items of memorabilia illustrating the history of the five regiments of Foot Guards in their service of sovereign and country in times of war and peace. Personal records of members of the Foot Guards are not part of the collection and access to them is not available through the museum.

Opening Hours: Daily 10am–4pm (last admissions 3.30pm).

Occasional closures on ceremonial days – please ring to avoid disappointment

Admission: Adults £4, seniors and students £2, children under 16 free. Groups and school parties by arrangement

Facilities: Restaurant, shop, disabled access, corporate events

HONOURABLE ARTILLERY COMPANY MUSEUM

Nearest Underground station is Moorgate

 Honourable Artillery Company Museum, Armoury House, City Road, London EC1Y 2BQ
T: 020 7382 1541 / F: 020 7382 1538
E: hac@hac.org.uk www.hac.uk.com

Archivist: Justine Taylor

The Company's museum is currently closed. The HAC has an extensive collection of uniforms and weapons. It also possesses a variety of shooting medals reflecting the Company's tradition of excellence in musketry dating from the early 19th century. Service medals are currently displayed in the Medal Room; the earliest medal sets – all donated by members and their families – date from the Boer War. The VCs won by two members of the Company at Gavrelle in 1917 are displayed in a separate cabinet. The HAC Archives and Library in Armoury House contain Company archives, private papers and books relating to the Company's history and warfare from the 17th century to the 21st Century. The Archives do not contain the formal service records of HAC members, although some information on membership is available. Enquiries to the Archivist are answered by email and post; personal visits to view items in the HAC Collections may be made by appointment in certain cases. There is no charge for research but a donation to the Archives Fund is requested. See the History and Archives pages of the HAC website for more information.

Opening Hours: The museum is currently closed for refurbishment.

Admission: Free. Donations welcome

Facilities: Toilets, disabled access, corporate events

HOUSEHOLD CAVALRY MUSEUM

Nearest Underground stations are Charing Cross, Embankment and Westminster

 Household Cavalry Museum, Horse Guards, Whitehall, London SW1A 2AX
T: 020 7930 3070
E: museum@householdcavalry.co.uk
www.householdcavalry.co.uk

Director: Martin Westwood

Life Guards, 1st Life Guards, 2nd Life Guards, Horse Grenadier Guards, Blues and Royals (Royal Horse Guards and 1st Dragoons), Royal Horse Guards (The Blues), Royal Horse Guards (Blue), King's or 1st Regiment of Horse, Royal Regiment of Horse (Oxford Blues)

The Household Cavalry Museum collections represent over 350 years of military history and reflect the unique ceremonial and operational role of the Regiment. These collections are displayed in a new museum, opened in June 2007 by HM The Queen, at Horse Guards. The museum gallery provides an introduction to the dual role of today's Household Cavalry regiments and traces their origins and historical development. Visitors also have the opportunity to see into the working stables block of The Queen's Life Guard and see behind the scenes of the Household Cavalry Mounted Regiment's daily contribution to public duties and State ceremonial.

The regimental archive remains at Combermere Barracks, Windsor SL2 3DN (Tel: 01753 755112). The archive, library, and education department forms part of a new collection resource facility that supports the Household Cavalry Museum in London.

Opening Hours: Open daily 10am–6pm Mar to Oct and 10am–5pm Nov to Feb. (except 24–26 Dec and Good Friday) Last admissions 45 mins before closing.

Admission: Adults £6, Children £4. Group discount if 10% for 8+. School party rates on request.

Facilities: Shop, toilets, disabled access

INNS OF COURT AND CITY YEOMANRY MUSEUM

Nearest Underground station is Chancery Lane

 Inns of Court and City Yeomanry Museum, 10 Stone Buildings, Lincoln's Inn, London WC2A 3TG
T: 020 7405 8112 / F: 020 7414 3496
E: iccy.li@virgin.net

Curator: Major Michael O'Beirne

A small collection housed in a classical George II building (1760 approx) in Lincoln's Inn recording the most unusual history of the Regiment and its predecessor units going back to 1584 when the members, all lawyers, were formed to defend London against the

All information is correct at the time of going to press, but **you are advised to contact museums before making a visit**

43

IMPERIAL WAR MUSEUM

IMPERIAL WAR **www.iwm.org.uk**

The Imperial War Museum is the national museum of the experiences of people who have lived, fought and died in conflicts involving Britain and the Commonwealth since 1914. The Museum provides visitors with an engaging programme of exhibitions and events across its five branches: IWM London, Churchill War Rooms in Whitehall, HMS Belfast moored on the River Thames, IWM Duxford in Cambridgeshire and IWM North in Manchester.

Director-General: Diane Lees

IMPERIAL WAR MUSEUM LONDON

Nearest Underground Station: Lambeth North, Nearest National Rail Station: Waterloo

Lambeth Road, London SE1 6HZ
T: 020 7416 5320/5321

Discover six floors of exhibitions and displays, which include the Explore History Centre where visitors can access the Museum's digital collections and a changing programme of special exhibitions.

Opening hours: Daily 10am–6pm (closed 24–26 Dec)

Admission: Free

CHURCHILL WAR ROOMS

Nearest Underground Station: Westminster

Clive Steps, King Charles Street, London SW1A 2AQ
T: 020 7930 6961

Learn more about the man who inspired Britain's finest hour at the highly interactive and innovative museum, and view the secret underground headquarters that was the nerve centre of Britain's war effort.

Opening hours: Daily 9.30am–6pm, last admission 5pm (closed 24–26 Dec)

Admission: £14.95 adults, £12.00 seniors and students; free to children under 16

HMS BELFAST

Nearest Underground Station and National Rail Station: London Bridge

Morgan's Lane, Tooley Street, London SE1 2JH
T: 020 7940 6300

Visit the largest surviving example of Britain's 20th-century naval power and explore over nine decks of history. Moored on the River Thames between London Bridge and Tower Bridge.

Opening hours: Daily Mar–Oct 10am–6pm, last admission 5pm. Nov–Feb 10am–5pm (closed 24–26 Dec)

Admission: £12.95 adults, £10.40 seniors and students; free to children under 16

IMPERIAL WAR MUSEUM DUXFORD

Duxford, Cambridgeshire CB2 4QR
T: 01223 835 000

Explore one of the world's finest aviation heritage sites which remains an active airfield. Visitors can see over 200 rare and historic aircraft including Spitfires, Concorde, Lancaster, Mustang and a Hurricane and enjoy a programme of air shows and special events throughout the year.

Opening hours: Daily 13 Mar to 23 Oct, 10am–6pm, last admission 5pm. 24 Oct to mid-Mar, 10am–4pm, last admission 3pm (closed 24–26 Dec)

Admission: £16.50 Adults, £13.20 Seniors and Students, free to children under 16

IMPERIAL WAR MUSEUM NORTH

The Quays, Trafford Wharf Road,
Trafford Park, Manchester M17 1TZ
T: 0161 836 4000

Visit the award-winning Museum to experience dynamic displays and thought-provoking temporary exhibitions.

Opening hours: Daily 1 Mar–1 Nov 10am–6pm, last admission 5.30pm; 2 Nov–28 Feb 10am- 5pm, last admission 4.30pm (closed 24–26 Dec)

Admission: Free

Directions for Travellers

Visit www.iwm.org.uk for directions to all five branches of the Imperial War Museum

threat of a Spanish invasion. Subsequently members took part in the English Civil War and the defence of the City during the Gordon Riots. Units were raised during the Napoleonic Wars and members fought during the Boer War and in later conflicts. It is the only regiment which had (and still has) a very close association with London's legal profession. In addition to uniforms, weapons, medals and memorabilia there is an excellent archive and possibly the oldest complete set of drums in the British Army, presented to the Law Association Volunteers in 1803.

Opening Hours: Mon–Fri 10am–4pm. By prior appointment only

Admission: Free, donations welcome. Groups and school parties by appointment

Facilities: Toilets. No disabled access

LONDON IRISH RIFLES MUSEUM **44**

London bus services 36, 185 and 436.
Nearest Underground station is Oval

London Irish Rifles Museum,
Connaught House, Flodden Road,
Camberwell, London SE5 9LL
T: 020 7820 4046 / F: 020 7820 4041
E:nwilkinson@googlemail.com
www.londonirishrifles.com

Curator: Captain (Retd) Nigel Wilkinson

A small collection of objects, medals and photographs reflecting the history of the Regiment from its foundation in 1859, through subsequent service in South Africa, the Western Front and Palestine in the Great War, as well as in Iraq, North Africa, Sicily and Italy in World War II. Among many other historic documents the collection includes the Roll of Honour from the Great War.

Opening Hours: By appointment only

Admission: Free

LONDON SCOTTISH REGIMENT MUSEUM **45**

Nearest Underground station is St James's Park

London Scottish Regiment Museum,
95 Horseferry Road, London SW1P 2DX
T: 020 7630 1639 / F: 020 7233 7909
E: regseclondonscot@aol.com
www.londonscottishregt.org/museum.cfm

Regimental Secretary:
Major Stuart Young
Regimental Archivist: John Wren

The small but comprehensive regimental collection is well displayed on two balconies in the drill hall at Regimental Headquarters. It includes uniforms, personal equipment, small arms, medals, paintings and other regimental memorabilia. The medals and uniform of Colonel Robert Ogilby, founder of the Army Museums Ogilby Trust, form part of the collection.

Opening Hours: By appointment only on Tue, Wed, and Thu 11.00am–4.00pm

Admission: Free, but donations to the London Scottish Benevolent Fund are welcomed

Facilities: Toilets, lecture room. Lift available but limited wheelchair access

NATIONAL ARMY MUSEUM *See p46* **46**

See p46

PRINCESS LOUISE'S KENSINGTON REGIMENT **47**

Nearest railway station is Coulsdon South

Princess Louise's Kensington Regiment Display Room
The TA Centre, Marlpit Lane,
Coulsdon, Surrey CR5 2HD
T: 01737 554023 / F: 01737 550298

Curator: Stephen Bland
(Tel: 020 8656 9740)

A small regimental collection that may be viewed by appointment only

ROYAL HOSPITAL MUSEUM **48**

Nearest Underground station is Sloane Square.
Buses, 19, 22, 211, 239, 319

Royal Hospital Museum,
Royal Hospital Chelsea,
Royal Hospital Road, London SW3 4SR
T: 020 7881 5203 / F: 020 7881 5463
E: info@chelsea-pensioners.org.uk
www.chelsea-pensioners.org.uk

Curator: Major Martin Snow

The home of the world famous Chelsea Pensioner since 1692, the Museum details the history and life of the Royal Hospital and its In-Pensioners together with displays of artefacts, documents, medals, cap badges and uniforms. Recent additions include the Sovereign's Mace and Parade Chair. A large diorama depicts the Royal Hospital and Ranelagh Pleasure gardens as they appeared in 1742.

Opening Hours: Mon–Sat 10am–12pm and 2pm–4pm. Sun 2pm–4pm (Apr–Sep only). Closed on Bank Holidays

Admission: Free

Facilities: Coach parking for party visits, toilets, shop

National Army Museum
Royal Hospital Road, Chelsea,
London SW3 4HT
T: 020 7730 0717
F: 020 7823 6573
E: info@national-army-museum.ac.uk
www.national-army-museum.ac.uk

Director: Janice Murray

LONDON

The National Army Museum traces the history of the British Army and its role in the making of Britain. The Museum's galleries examine the history of the British Army through the ages, from the Norman Conquest right up until the present day in its Conflicts of Interest gallery. Its collection is a treasure trove of artefacts and archives that touch on events ranging from those of national and international importance, such as the American War of Independence or the current conflict in Afghanistan, to the conditions of life as a National Serviceman or an archer at Agincourt. The difficult and dangerous life of the British soldier and the changing world in which he has lived throughout the centuries is brought to life by interactive sound and visual displays. The galleries also address wider themes such as the control and organization of the Army, the daily life of the soldier and civilian perceptions of the Army.

The Museum presents regular special exhibitions, events, celebrity speakers and lunchtime lectures; full details of which can be found on the Museum's website. The Museum also has Action Zones and a Kids' Zone that provide hands-on activities for kids aged 0–10.

The Museum boasts a variety of research and study tools to enable visitors to delve into its collections further. The Templer Study Centre (open 10am-5pm Wednesday, Thursday and Friday, and the first and third Saturday of every month) offers readers the chance to access regimental and campaign histories, archives, photographs, prints and drawings.

Encompassing Militia, Yeomanry, Volunteers and the Territorial Army as well as the regular forces, the museum also looks at the armies of the British Empire and Commonwealth during the two world wars and tells the history of the Indian Army up to 1947. The collections of the pre-1922 Irish regiments of the British Army are dispersed amongst the collection as a whole. In addition the museum is home to the regimental collections of:

The Buffs, 3rd Regiment of Foot, Royal East Kent Regiment, The Middlesex Regiment, 57th (or the West Middlesex) Regiment of Foot, 77th (The East Middlesex) Regiment of Foot (Duke of Cambridge's Own), 77th Regiment of Foot, Women's Royal Army Corps, Auxiliary Training Service, Women's Army Auxiliary Corps.

Opening Hours: Daily 10am–5.30pm. Closed 24–26 Dec, 1 Jan, Good Friday, early May Bank Holiday

Admission: Free

Facilities: Parking, toilets, restaurant, shop, disabled access, library and research facilities, Society of Friends, hospitality packages, birthday parties, e-commerce

Directions for Travellers

Nearest Mainline railway station: Victoria

Nearest Underground station: Sloane Square

*Buses: Nos 11, 19, 22 and 211 to King's Road
            No 137, 156 and 360 to Pimlico Road
            No 170 stops outside the Museum*

ROYAL MILITARY SCHOOL OF MUSIC MUSEUM 49

Underground to Hounslow East, then by bus along B361 or by car along A316 (next to Twickenham rugby ground)

 Royal Military School of Music Museum, Kneller Hall, Twickenham, Middlesex TW2 7DU
T: 020 8744 8652 / F: 020 8744 8652
E: corpssec@hq.dcamus.mod.uk

Curator: Major JH Carter

The collection consists mainly of musical instruments used by military bands since 1780, plus uniforms, paintings and associated objects. The archive is housed in the Curator's office and may be viewed by appointment.

Opening Hours: Weekdays by appointment only (normally on Wednesday mornings during May–Aug)

Admission: Adults £4 (guided tour), Students £3, Children under 12 £2.

Facilities: Parking, café, toilets, limited disabled access

ROYAL REGIMENT OF FUSILIERS (LONDON) MUSEUM 50

Nearest Underground station is Tower Hill. Buses 15, 42, 78

 Royal Regiment of Fusiliers (London) Museum, HM Tower of London, London EC3N 4AB
T: 0203 166 6910 / F: 020 7481 1093
E: royalfusiliers@fsmail.net

Curator: Major Colin Bowes-Crick

Royal Fusiliers (City of London Regiment), 7th Regiment of Foot (or the Royal Fuziliers), Royal Regiment of Fusiliers (or Ordnance Regiment)

The collection of the Royal Fusiliers (City of London Regiment) covering its history from 1685 to 1968 and of the Royal Regiment of Fusiliers from 1968 onwards. The exhibits include uniforms, weapons, equipment, colours and dioramas of the battles of Albuhera, Mons and Cassino.

Research inquiries are accepted by post only and must be accompanied by a SAE.

Opening Hours: Summer weekdays 9.30am–5.15pm, Sun 10.30am–5.15pm. Winter weekdays 9.30am–4.15pm, Sun 10.30am–5.15pm. **The museum will be closed from 1st Oct 2010 to 1st March 2011 inclusive for major refurbishment.**

Admission: Free after payment of entry charge to HM Tower of London.

WESTMINSTER DRAGOONS MUSEUM 51

Nearest Underground station is Putney Bridge

 W (Westminster Dragoons) Squadron, Fulham House, 87 Fulham High Street, London SW6 3JS
T: 020 7384 4201
E: ry-w-psao@mod.uk
www.westminsterdragoons.co.uk

Curator: Major Jeremy Gambles

A small private collection relating to the Westminster Dragoons.

The collection is currently in storage during the refurbishment of premises and re-opening is not anticipated before 2011.

Email correspondence with the curator will be forwarded from the address shown.

Opening Hours: By appointment only

Admission: Free

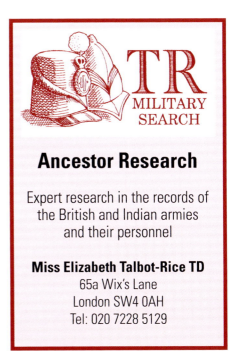

East Anglia

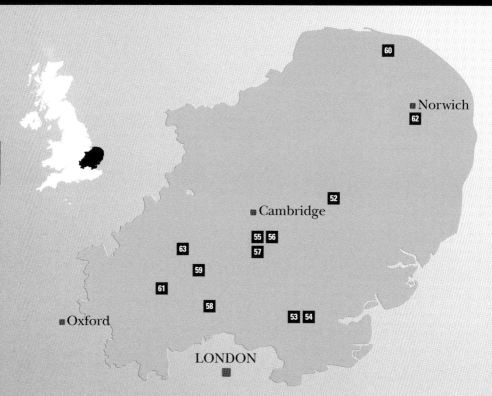

EAST ANGLIA

Bury St Edmunds

THE SUFFOLK REGIMENT MUSEUM

Suffolk Regiment Museum, The Keep, Gibraltar Barracks, Newmarket Road, Bury St Edmunds, Suffolk IP33 3RN
T: 01284 752394
E: taff@taffmail.demon.co.uk
www.suffolkregiment.org/Museum.html

Curator: Gwyn Thomas

Royal Anglian Regiment, The Suffolk Regiment, 12th (or East Suffolk) Regiment of Foot, 12th Regiment of Foot, Duke of Norfolk's Regiment of Foot, Cambridgeshire Regiment TA

Following extensive renovation and refurbishment, the museum houses a well-presented, comprehensive collection of objects associated with the County Regiment of Suffolk. The collection includes displays of uniforms, weapons, regimental trophies from its many campaigns in the service of the Crown, badges, insignia, musical items and regimental memorabilia.

The Regimental Archive is held by the Suffolk County Records Office, Tel 01284.352352.

Opening Hours: First and third Wednesday of each month 9.30am–3.30pm and first Sunday of each month 9.30am–3.30pm throughout the year

Admission: Free, donations welcome

Facilities: Parking, toilets, shop

Chelmsford

ESSEX REGIMENT MUSEUM

SSW of town just off A1016, or buses 152, 154, 350, 351, 42 and 44 from town centre and railway station

Essex Regiment Museum,
Oaklands Park, Moulsham Street, Chelmsford, Essex CM2 9AQ
T: 01245 605700 / F: 01245 262428
E: pompadour@chelmsford.gov.uk
www.chelmsfordbc.gov.uk/museums

Curator: Ian Hook

Royal Anglian Regiment, 3rd East Anglian Regiment, Essex Regiment, 44th (or the East Essex) Regiment of Foot, 44th Regiment of Foot, Colonel Long's Regiment of Foot, 56th (or the West Essex) Regiment of Foot, 56th Regiment of Foot, Essex Militia, Rifles, Rifle Volunteer and Volunteer units, Essex Yeomanry Cavalry, Essex Artillery Volunteers, Essex and Suffolk Royal Garrison Artillery, Essex (Fortress) Royal Engineers, Essex Local Defence Volunteers, Essex Home Guard

New Museum and Essex Yeomanry Display opened in January 2010.

The regimental collection, housed in an extension to the Chelmsford Museum, is an impressive display of well-presented exhibits tracing the history of the Regiment from 1741 to the present day. Uniforms, trophies – including the Salamanca Eagle captured from the French 62nd Regiment – badges, insignia, weapons and regimental memorabilia reflect the worldwide service of the Essex Regiment in the service of the Crown. Access to a comprehensive family history database is available by appointment, letter or email, for which a donation to The Trustees of the Essex Regiment Museum is appreciated.

The museum also houses the collection of the **Essex Yeomanry** whose history and other details are available from their website (www.essex-yeomanry.org.uk)

Opening Hours: Mon–Sat 10am–5pm. Sun 1pm–4pm

Admission: Free. Groups and school parties by appointment

Facilities: Parking, toilets, shop, disabled access, education service. Tea, coffee and soft drinks available.

Duxford

AIRBORNE ASSAULT – MUSEUM OF THE PARACHUTE REGIMENT AND AIRBORNE FORCES

IWM Duxford is 5 miles south of Cambridge just off the M11 at Junction 10

Museum of the Parachute Regiment and Airborne Forces
Building 213, North Base, Imperial War Museum Duxford, Cambridge, CB22 4QR
T: 01223 839909
E: airborne.enquiries@btconnect.com
www.paradata.org.uk

Curator: Jonathan Baker

Parachute Regiment, Airborne Forces, Glider Pilot Regiment, No 2 Commando, 11 SAS

Located in the spectacular AirSpace gallery, Airborne Assault tells the story of men who go to war from the air. Using weapons, equipment, medals, uniforms, and multi-media techniques it celebrates the heritage of today's airborne soldiers. The full history of The Parachute Regiment and Airborne Forces is dramatically depicted, from inception by Churchill in 1940, through actions in Africa, Sicily, Suez, Borneo, the Falklands, Iraq, to present-day operations in Afghanistan. Highlights include: original World War II briefing models from Normandy, Pegasus Bridge, Rhine Crossing and Bruneval; a Horsa glider nose cone; heavy drop equipment; and Bing the Paradog, who dropped in Operation Varsity, 1945. The new conservation-standard archive, with full facilities for historians and researchers, is also housed separately on the Duxford site. ParaData, the definitive digital database of men, units, operations, campaigns, photographs, film and memorabilia of Airborne Forces is accessible through touch screens at the museum and online through the internet.

Opening Hours: Daily except Dec 24, 25, 26. 10am–4pm in Winter and 9am–5pm in Summer. Please see www.iwm.org.uk website for season dates.

Admission: Entry to IWM includes entry to the Museum of the Parachute Regiment and Airborne Forces. Full tariff at www.iwm.org.uk concessions available to groups of cadets, serving soldiers and PRA members by prior appointment with Curator. Details on website and through Curator.

Facilities: Parking, toilets, restaurant/café, shop, disabled access, lecture room

CAMBRIDGESHIRE REGIMENT COLLECTION

As for Royal Anglian Regiment Museum below

The Cambridgeshire Regiment Collection is a small but well presented display of items associated with the County's volunteer infantry regiment. It is housed adjacent to the Royal Anglian Regiment Museum and all details are as shown below.

ROYAL ANGLIAN REGIMENT MUSEUM

By road, leave M11 at J10 or take Royston-Newmarket road. Courtesy buses run from Cambridge railway station and Crowne Plaza to Imperial War Museum Duxford. There is also a daily express service from Victoria

Royal Anglian Regiment Museum,
Land Warfare Hall, Imperial War Museum, Duxford, Cambridge CB22 4QR
T: 01223 497298
E: info@royalanglianmuseum.org.uk
www.royalanglianmuseum.org.uk

Curator: Andy Murkin

Royal Anglian Regiment, 1st East Anglian Regiment (Royal Norfolk and Suffolk), 2nd East Anglian Regiment (Duchess of Gloucester's Own; Royal Lincolnshire and Northamptonshire), 3rd East Anglian Regiment (16th/44thFoot), Royal Leicestershire Regiment

The collection covers the history of the Royal Anglian Regiment since its formation in 1958 which resulted from the amalgamation of the former County Regiments of East Anglia and the East Midlands. The several amalgamations which preceded today's regiment date back to 1685 and are well illustrated in a detailed family tree. Exhibits include uniforms, weapons, badges and displays dedicated to particular operations on which the regiment has been deployed.

Opening Hours: Summer 10am–6pm daily.
Winter 10am–4pm daily.

Admission: Free after payment of entrance fee to the Imperial War Museum

Facilities: Parking, toilets, refreshments, shop, disabled access, lecture room

Notes
1. Admission charges include access to the whole of the Imperial War Museum Duxford. 2. Different admission prices apply for Air Shows and some special events. 3. See www.iwm.org.uk for details of current charges and changes to opening hours.

COMBINED MILITARY SERVICES MUSEUM

Station Road, Maldon
Essex CM9 4LQ
T: 01621 841826.
E: admin@cmsmc.co.uk
www.cmsm.co.uk

The Museum houses a collection of British military artefacts that illustrate changes in the British armed forces from medieval times to present day. Many of the items on display are of national importance.

A good example is the only surviving MK2 'Cockle' canoe, believed to be the sixth canoe Cachalot, which was damaged whilst being taken through the hatch of HMS Tuna and subsequently returned to England, and other equipment used in the 'Cockleshell Heroes' raid.

There is an excellent Civil War collection, including the Biglands English Civil War Collection – a unique collection of English Civil War arms and armour. Amongst the artefacts is an extremely rare example of a Cavalier's felt hat and buff waistcoat thought to be some of the only surviving examples in existence.

Manikin displays cover all the armed forces and show many rare original webbing and equipment sets not seen elsewhere. Examples include paratroopers from Arnhem, Suez and the Falklands. Commandos, SAS and SOE agents line the display cases alongside RAF pilots from World War I to the Gulf War.

The museum also holds a fine sword collection and clandestine weapons collection.

External exhibits include a Chieftain Tank, Iraqi T69 Tank and armoured Personnel Carrier, captured during the First Gulf War, and a Thunderbird Missile.

The Spy Collection

The Museum houses one of the largest collections of spy equipment on public display in the world. This is the unique and fascinating collection of espionage equipment from former British Agents Captain Peter Mason and his wife Prue Mason. Step into the world of James Bond and view spy gadgets – but unlike the Bond world, these are real.

Donnington Firearms Collection

This collection is one of the finest firearm collections on public display in Europe. Assembled by MOD Donnington in the second half of the 20th century. The collection consists of weapons used and captured by the British Army during the late 19th and 20th centuries which builds a picture of the operations and experiences of the Army that is not available anywhere else.

The Museum was awarded best exhibition for its Spy collection, and Best Museum in Essex 2009.

Group bookings can be arranged for evenings, when the Museum is closed to the public. We also organise special themed events, presentations and demonstrations on specialised subjects.

School visits are actively encouraged, and we will assist in providing activity sheets and support as required to minimise teacher workload.

Opening Hours:
Wed–Sun 10.30–5pm Open Bank Holiday Mondays and everyday during school holidays.

Admission:

Adult (under 16)	£4.75
Child (under 5 free	£3.00
Concession (60+)	£3.75
Family ticket (2 adults 3 children)	£15.50

Registered Charity No. 1058595

Hertford

HERTFORDSHIRE REGIMENT MUSEUM 58

Close to town centre and public parking. Nearest station is Hertford East

Hertfordshire Regiment Museum Collection, Hertford Museum, 18 Bull Plain, Hertford SG14 1DT
T: 01922 582686
E: hertfordmuseum@btconnect.com
www.hertfordmuseum.org

Curator: Helen Gurney

Re-opened in 2010 after extensive refurbishment the museum houses a small regimental collection on the 1st floor. The display includes uniforms, medals, silver and other regimental memorabilia.

Opening Hours: Tue–Sat 10am–5pm

Admission: Free

Facilities: Toilets, shop, disabled access

Hitchin

HERTFORDSHIRE YEOMANRY AND ARTILLERY COLLECTION 59

Along A505 Hitchin-Luton road or A600 Hitchin-Bedford road

Hertfordshire Yeomanry and Artillery Collection, Hitchin Museum, Paynes Park, Hitchin, Hertfordshire SG5 1EH
T. 01462 434476 F. 01462 431316
E. david.hodges@north-herts.gov.uk
www.north-herts.gov.uk

Curator: David Hodges

A small collection of uniforms, badges, weapons and medals of the Yeomanry and Artillery units raised in Hertfordshire from 1794 to modern times. The associated archives are held at the Hertfordshire Archives and Local Studies Centre, County Hall, Hertford SG13 8DE

Opening Hours: Mon–Sat (except Wed) 10am–5pm. Closed Sun, Wed and public holidays

Admission: Free

Facilities: Parking, shop, disabled access

Holt

SUFFOLK AND NORFOLK YEOMANRY COLLECTION 60

Off the main A149 coast road four miles west of Sheringham

Suffolk and Norfolk Yeomanry Collection, The Muckleburgh Collection, Weybourne, Holt, Norfolk NR25 7EH
T: 01263 588210 / F: 01263 588425
E: info@muckleburgh.co.uk
www.muckleburgh.co.uk

Curator: Michael Savory

A small regimental collection, set within a much larger display of weapons, vehicles and equipment totalling some 3,000 objects, traces the history of the Regiment from the raising of the Norfolk Rangers in 1782 to the present day. It includes some fine early uniforms, helmets and regimental banners, the first of which dates from the reign of George III and has a rare example of the 2 PDR anti-tank guns which saw service with the Regiment in World War II.

Opening Hours: Apr–Oct 10am–5pm daily.
Last admissions at 4pm.

Admission: Adults £6, Seniors and HM Forces £5, Children £4 (under 5's free), Family ticket £17. Groups and school parties by appointment

Facilities: Parking, toilets, shop, disabled access

Luton

BEDFORDSHIRE AND HERTFORDSHIRE REGIMENT MUSEUM

1 mile north of town centre

Bedfordshire and Hertfordshire Regiment Museum Collection, Wardown Museum, Wardown Park, Luton, Bedfordshire LU2 7HA
T: 01582 546722/546725 / F: 01582 546763
E: Elizabeth.adey@lutonculture.com
www.wardownparkmuseum.com

Curatorial Advisor: Elizabeth Adey

Bedfordshire and Hertfordshire Regiment, Bedfordshire Regiment, 16th (or Bedfordshire) Regiment of Foot, 16th (or Buckinghamshire) Regiment of Foot, 16th Regiment of Foot, Colonel Douglas's Regiment of Foot

Within Wardown Museum, a gallery devoted to the regimental collection of the County Regiment and its predecessors. Bedfordshire and Luton Archives and Records Service holds the Regimental Archives. For family history enquiries contact Nigel Lutt on 01234 228833, or email Nigel.Lutt@Bedscc.gov.uk

Opening Hours: Tue–Sat: 10am–5pm, Sun 1pm–5pm. Closed 25–26 Dec and 1 Jan

Admissions: Free

Facilities: Parking, toilets, refreshments, shop, disabled access

Norwich

ROYAL NORFOLK REGIMENT MUSEUM

Town centre location on the east side of the Castle Mound

Royal Norfolk Regiment Museum, Shirehall, Market Avenue, Norwich, Norfolk NR1 3JQ
T: 01603 493649 / F: 01603 493623
E: regimental.museum@norfolk.gov.uk
www.rnrm.org.uk

Curator: Kate Thaxton

Royal Anglian Regiment, Royal Norfolk Regiment, Norfolk Regiment 9th (or East Norfolk) Regiment of Foot, 9th Regiment of Foot, Colonel Henry Cornwall's Regiment of Foot

The Regiment was formed in 1685 and served around the world. The museum tells its story and the part that Norfolk's soldiers, and their families, played in shaping three centuries of global history. The displays are themed and arranged chronologically, with excellent interpretative panels; designed for those with no military knowledge as well as the military historian.

Opening Hours: Tue–Sat 10am–4.30pm.
High season: 28 June–3 October, Tue–Sat 10am–5pm

Admission: Adults £3.50, Seniors £2.90, Children £1.90, Family ticket £9.10. Groups and school parties by appointment.

Facilities: Shop, toilets, adjacent car parking.
Archives by appointment.

Shefford

MILITARY INTELLIGENCE MUSEUM

Off A600 between Bedford and Shefford, sign-posted 'Chicksands'

The Military Intelligence Museum, Defence Intelligence and Security Centre, Chicksands, Shefford, Bedfordshire SG17 5PR
T: 01462 752896
F: 01462 752374
E: reed093@disc.mod.uk
www2.armynet.mod.uk/museums/intelligence

Curator: Sally Ann Reed

The collections of The Military Intelligence Museum include the Intelligence Corps Museum which charts the development of British Military Intelligence along with the Medmenham Collection highlighting the important role of aerial imagery. Combined with this is the BRIXMIS Collection – telling the story of Intelligence gathering in East Germany at the height of the Cold War. Finally there is the story of Chicksands – including its use inorld War II as a 'Y' Service intercept station of Enigma Codes and its post-war USAF intelligence gathering activities up to the late 1990s. A varied and interesting collection allowing you to 'Share the Secret…'

Opening Hours: By appointment only. We are open from 10am to 2pm Monday to Thursday (all are welcome) but PLEASE telephone first

Admission: Free

Facilities: Parking, toilets, shop

Wales

Brecon

THE ROYAL WELSH (BRECON) MUSEUM

By regular bus service from Abergavenny, Newport and Merthyr Tydfil railway stations. Museum is next to Brecon Barracks on B4601

Royal Regiment of Wales (Brecon) Museum,
The Barracks, Brecon,
Powys LD3 7EB
T: 01874 613310 / F: 01874 613275
E: swb@rrw.org.uk
www.rrw.org.uk

Curator: Major Martin Everett

The Royal Welsh, Royal Regiment of Wales (24th/41st Foot), South Wales Borderers, 24th (2nd Warwickshire) Regiment of Foot, 24th Regiment of Foot, Sir Edward Dering's Regiment of Foot, The Monmouthshire Regiment, Brecknockshire, Radnorshire, Montgomeryshire and Monmouthshire Militia and Volunteers Regiments

The regimental collections of the South Wales Borderers and the Monmouthshire Regiment are the focus of well-presented displays in this fine regimental museum. Of particular interest are the exhibits covering the activities of the Regiment in the 1879 Anglo-Zulu War including the 24th's heroic defence of Rorke's Drift. The medal room contains nearly 3,500 medals, and the sixteen Victoria Crosses won by members of the Regiment form an impressive central display. The regimental archive and library are on the same site and may be viewed by appointment with the Curator. The museum also houses the archives of 41st (Welch) Foot; 69th (South Lincolnshire) Foot; The Welch Regiment; and some material of the Pembrokeshire and Glamorganshire Yeomanries

Opening Hours: Mon–Fri throughout the year, 10am–5pm. Summer: Sat and Bank Holidays 10am–4pm. See website or contact the museum for details of special Sunday openings

Admission: Adults £3, Children (16 and under) free. Group rates are negotiable. School parties by appointment.

Facilities: Parking, toilets, shop, disabled access, lecture room

Caernarfon

ROYAL WELCH FUSILIERS MUSEUM

A55 from Chester or A487 from South and Mid Wales and follow signs to the museum. By rail to Bangor and then bus or taxi to Caernarfon

 Royal Welch Fusiliers Museum,
The Castle, Caernarfon, Gwynedd LL55 2AY
T: 01286 673362 / F: 01286 677042
E: rwfusiliers@callnetuk.com
www.rwfmuseum.org.uk

Curator: Brian Owen

The Royal Welsh, Royal Welch Fusiliers, Royal Welsh Fusiliers, 23rd Regiment of Foot (Royal Welsh Fusiliers), Royal Regiment of Welsh Fusiliers, Prince of Wales's Own Royal Welsh Fuziliers, Welsh Regiment of Fuziliers, Lord Herbert of Chirbury's Regiment of Foot, Herbert's Regiment, Purcell's Regiment, Morgan's Regiment, Ingoldsby's Regiment, Sabine's Regiment, Peer's Regiment, Huske's Regiment, Denbighshire Hussars Yeomanry, Montgomeryshire Hussars Yeomanry

The collection covers the 300-year history of Wales's oldest infantry regiment and occupies five floors in two towers of the castle. There are fine displays of uniforms, medals and regimental memorabilia from the many campaigns in which it has fought. There is also reference to the Regiment's famous World War I literary heritage linked to Robert Graves, Siegfried Sassoon, David Jones, Frank Richards and Dr Dunn. The regimental library and archive are not held on site and may be viewed by appointment only.

Opening Hours: Mar–Jun 9.30am–5pm, Jul–Aug 9.30am–6.00pm, Sept–Oct 9.30am–5.00pm, Nov–Mar 10am–4pm Mon to Sat. 11am–4pm Sun

Admission: Free with entry to Caernarfon Castle: Adults £4.90, Concessions £4.50, Family ticket £15

Facilities: Adjacent parking, toilets, shop

Cardiff

FIRING LINE: CARDIFF MUSEUM OF THE WELSH SOLDIER

City centre location near railway stations, bus services and car parking

Firing Line: Cardiff Museum of the Welsh Soldier
The Castle, Cardiff, South Glamorgan CF10 2RB
T: 029 2022 9367
E: curator@cardiffcastlemuseum.org.uk
www.cardiffcastlemuseum.org.uk

Curator: Rachel Silverson
Deputy: Clive Morris

The Royal Welsh, Royal Regiment of Wales, The Welch Regiment (41st/69th Foot), 41st (The Welsh) Regiment of Foot, 41st Regiment of Foot or Invalids, 41st (Royal Invalids) Regiment, Colonel Fielding's Regiment of Foot, 69th (South Lincolnshire) Regiment of Foot, 1st The Queen's Dragoon Guards, 1st King's Dragoon Guards, 2nd Dragoon Guards (Queen's Bays), 2nd (Queen's) Dragoon Guards, 2nd or Queen's Regiment of Dragoons, 1st of King's Regiment of Dragoon Guards, Queen's or 2nd Regiment of Horse, Queen's Own Royal Regiment of Horse, Princess of Wales's Own Royal Regiment of Horse, King's Regiment of Horse, 2nd Horse, 3rd Regiment of Horse (Peterborough's), Queen's Regiment of Horse.

This new museum opened in March 2010. The collection covers the history of services of the 41st and 69th Regiments of Foot from 1719 until 1969 when The Welch Regiment amalgamated with others to form The Royal Regiment of Wales and in 2006 became The Royal Welsh. The 41st Foot was originally formed of Out Pensioners from the Royal Hospital Chelsea and titled Sir Edmund Fielding's Regiment of Invalids. In 1787 the title Invalids was abandoned and the 41st became a marching Regiment of The Line. In 1881 it was joined by the 69th Regiment of Foot and became The Welch Regiment.

The joint exhibition also includes the regimental collection of 1st the Queens Dragoon Guards. This reflects the long history of Wales's only regular cavalry regiment, 1st The Queen's Dragoon Guards which began its formal existence on 1 January 1959, this being the day when the 1st King's Dragoon Guards was amalgamated with the 2nd Dragoon Guards, better known as the Queen's Bays.

Opening Hours: Daily 9am–5pm including Bank Holidays. Closed Christmas Day, Boxing Day and New Year's Day

Admission: Charges are included in Castle entry fees:
Castle Premium Tours: Adult £13.50, Child £10.00, Senior £11.50
Castle Essential Tours: Adult £10.50, Child £7.95, Senior £9.00

Facilities: Toilets, restaurant, shop, lecture room.

Carmarthen

CARMARTHEN MILITIA AND VOLUNTEERS COLLECTION

Museum located on A40, 1.5 miles east of Carmarthen

Carmarthen Militia and Volunteers Collection, Carmarthen County Museum, Abergwili, Carmarthen, Carmarthenshire SA31 2JG
T: 01267 228696 / F: 01267 223830
E: museums@carmarthenshire.gov.uk

Curator: Gavin Evans

A small display of objects associated with the local Yeomanry Cavalry, Militia and Volunteer units.

Opening Hours: Mon–Sat 10am–4.30pm

Admission: Free. Groups and school parties by appointment

Facilities: Parking, toilets, refreshments, shop, disabled access, education service

Haverfordwest

PEMBROKE YEOMANRY COLLECTION

By car, A40 or M4/A48/A40, then 4 miles north on B4329. By coach or train to Haverfordwest

Pembroke Yeomanry Collection, Scolton Manor Museum, Spittal, Haverfordwest, Pembrokeshire SA62 5QL
T: 01437 731328 / F: 01437 731743

Curator: Mark Thomas / Catriona Hilditch

The Collection includes uniforms and accoutrements of the Pembroke Yeomanry, Royal Pembroke Militia, Pembroke Volunteers and associated regiments. Items are not on permanent display but can be viewed by appointment. There is also a World War II Gallery. Archives are held at the Haverfordwest County Record Office.

Opening Hours: Sun–Mon from 1 Apr to 31 Oct, 10.30am–5.30pm

Admission: Adults £2, Children £1, concessions £1.50, Seniors £1. Groups and school parties by appointment

Facilities: Parking, toilets, refreshments, shop, lecture room

Monmouth

ROYAL MONMOUTHSHIRE ROYAL ENGINEERS (MILITIA) MUSEUM

At the highest point of the town, behind Woolworth's. Rail and bus links are poor

Royal Monmouthshire Royal Engineers Museum Collection, Castle and Regimental Museum, The Castle, Monmouth NP25 3BS
T: 01600 772175
E: curator@monmouthcastlemuseum.org.uk
www.monmouthcastlemuseum.org.uk

Hon. Administrator: Eric Old

Royal Monmouthshire Royal Engineers (Militia), Royal Monmouthshire (Light Infantry) Militia

The museum of the Senior Regiment of the Reserve Army – the sole survivor of the Militia – covers the history of the Regiment from its initial mustering in 1539. Displays include uniforms, weapons, insignia, medals, drawings, books and documents. Coverage of the Regiment's recent activities includes exhibits related to operations in Iraq. The Regimental archives may be viewed by appointment.

Opening Hours: 1 Apr–31 Oct (including Easter), 2pm–5pm daily At other times by appointment.

Admission: Free. Donations welcome. Groups and school parties by appointment

Facilities: Sales counter, disabled access

WALES

Tenby

CASTLEMARTIN YEOMANRY COLLECTION

Town centre location

Castlemartin Yeomanry Collection, Tenby Museum and Art Gallery, Castle Hill, Tenby, Pembrokeshire SA70 7BP
T: 01834 842809 / F: 01834 842809
E: info@tenbymuseum.org.uk

Curator: Kathy Talbot

Within a general collection of items relating to the local area there is a small collection of objects associated with the Castlemartin Troop of the Pembroke Yeomanry Cavalry and Pembroke Cavalry (Castlemartin) (Hussars). Currently on display is a sword taken from one of the French invaders at Fishguard in 1797. At present the remainder of the Collection is not on public display but is accessible by appointment. Research facilities are available.

Opening Hours: Summer: 10am–5pm daily. Winter: 10am–5pm Mon–Fri (Last admissions 4.30pm)

Admission: Adults £4, Concession £3, Children £2, Family ticket £9. Groups and school parties by appointment

Facilities: Toilets, coffee shop, shop, disabled access, lecture room, education seervice, bilingual audio tour

Welshpool

MONTGOMERYSHIRE YEOMANRY COLLECTION

On main road, 5 minutes from the station

Montgomeryshire Yeomanry Museum Collection, Powysland Museum, The Canal Wharf, Welshpool, Powys SY21 7AQ
T: 01938 554656
E: powysland@powys.gov.uk

Curator: Eva Bredsdorff

A small collection of items related to the Montgomeryshire Yeomanry within a local museum of archaeology and social history.

Opening Hours: Summer: weekdays 11am–1pm and 2pm–5pm. Closed Wed; weekends 10am–1pm and 2pm–5pm
Winter: Sat only 11am–2pm

Admission: Adults £1, Seniors 50p, Children free. Groups and school parties by appointment. Powys residents free

Facilities: Disabled access and adjacent parking for disabled visitors

WAL

Hereford:	**72**	Herefordshire Light Infantry
Lichfield:	**73**	Staffordshire Regiment
Shrewsbury:	**74**	Shropshire Regimental Museum
Stafford:	**75**	Staffordshire Yeomanry
Warwick:	**76**	Queen's Own Hussars
	77	Royal Regiment of Fusiliers (Royal Warwickshire)
	78	Warwickshire Yeomanry
Worcester:	**79**	Worcestershire Regiment
	80	Worcestershire Yeomanry

Hereford

HEREFORDSHIRE LIGHT INFANTRY MUSEUM `72`

Southeast of the city off the Ledbury road and B4224

Herefordshire Light Infantry Museum,
TA Centre, Harold Street,
Hereford HR1 2QX
T: 01432 359917
E: ameshereford@waitrose.com

Curator: James Hereford

*Herefordshire Light Infantry, Herefordshire Regiment,
Herefordshire Rifle Volunteer Corps, Herefordshire Militia*

A small collection of objects associated with the regiments raised in Herefordshire dating from the Volunteers of the Napoleonic period.

Opening Hours: Mon–Fri 9.30am–4pm. By appointment only

Admission: Free

Facilities: Parking, toilets, disabled access

Lichfield

STAFFORDSHIRE REGIMENT MUSEUM `73`

*On A51 Lichfield-Tamworth road next to Whittington Barracks.
Bus no 765 stops outside*

Staffordshire Regiment Museum,
Whittington Barracks, Lichfield,
Staffordshire WS14 9PY
T: 01543 434394/5 / F: 01543 434391
E: curator@staffordshire
regimentmuseum.com
http://x.staffordshire
regimentmuseum.com

Curator: Dr Erik Blakeley

Staffordshire Regiment (Prince of Wales's), South Staffordshire Regiment, 38th (or 1st Staffordshire) Regiment of Foot, 38th Regiment of Foot, Colonel Lillington's Regiment of Foot, North Staffordshire Regiment (Prince of Wales's), 64th (or 2nd Staffordshire) Regiment of Foot, 64th Regiment of Foot, 80th (or Staffordshire Volunteers) Regiment of Foot, 80th Regiment of Foot, 98th (Prince of Wales's) Regiment of Foot, 98th Regiment of Foot

The collection tells the story of the Regiment and its forbears from its formation in Lichfield in 1705. It includes uniforms, equipment, medals (8 of the Regiment's 13 VCs are on display), badges and regimental memorabilia. There are special sections covering Militia and Volunteers, the Zulu War, both world wars and the Gulf War. There is a children's hands-on area and outside there are armoured vehicles, two Anderson Shelters and a long section of WW1

trench. The Regimental archive and library are on-site and may be viewed by appointment. The Museum runs excellent school visits which are linked to the National Curriculum, runs several imaginative military re-enactor events at weekends throughout the year – including Redcoats, WW1, WW2, even Carols in the Trenches. The Museum regularly features in the Midlands News

Opening Hours: Mon–Fri 10am–4.30pm all year.
Apr–Remembrance Sunday, Sat, Sun and Bank Holidays 12.30pm–4.30 pm

Admission: Adults £3. Concessions £2, Children £2 (under 5s free), Family ticket £6. School parties £2.50 per pupil.

Note: Special Events are in aid of the Staffordshire Regiment Museum Charitable Trust and higher special event prices may apply on these occasions

Facilities: Parking, toilets, shop, disabled access, research facilities, picnic area

Shrewsbury

SHROPSHIRE REGIMENTAL MUSEUM `74`

100 yards from main bus and railway stations

Shropshire Regimental Museum Trust,
The Castle, Shrewsbury,
Shropshire SY1 2AT
T: 01743 262292 / F: 01743 270023
E: shropshireregiments@tiscali.co.uk
www.shropshireregiments.org.uk

Curator: Peter Duckers

King's Shropshire Light Infantry, King's (Shropshire Light Infantry), King's Light Infantry, 53rd (or the Shropshire) Regiment of Foot, 53rd Regiment of Foot, 85th King's Light Infantry, 85th (Bucks Volunteers) (The King's Light Infantry), 85th (Bucks Volunteers) (Duke of York's Own Light Infantry), 85th (Bucks Volunteers)(Light Infantry) Regiment, 85th (Bucks Volunteers) Regiment of Foot, 85th (Westminster Volontiers) Regiment of Foot, 85th Light Infantry Regiment or Royal Volontiers, Crauford's Regiment of Foot, Shropshire Rifle Volunteers, Shropshire Militia, Shropshire Royal Horse Artillery, Shropshire Yeomanry, Queen's Own Mercian Yeomanry

A very rich collection of artefacts, conventionally displayed on 3 floors in a medieval border castle, covering the history of the King's Shropshire Light Infantry and the County's Artillery, Yeomanry, Militia, Volunteer and Territorial units.

Opening Hours: 1 May to 12 September, six days per week, 10am–5pm (closed Thurs) 12 Sept to 20 Dec and mid-Feb to 1 May, 10am–4pm (closed Sun and Thurs)

Admission: Free to all ex-members of the regiments represented and their families, Borough residents, all children and students and ex-Shropshire regimental members. Otherwise Adults £2.50 and Concessions £1.25

Facilities: Toilets, shop, disabled access to both main floors

Stafford

STAFFORDSHIRE YEOMANRY MUSEUM

A 10-minute walk from the station. By car exit M6 at J13 then A449 or J14 then A34

Staffordshire Yeomanry Museum,
The Ancient High House,
Greengate Street, Stafford ST16 2JA
T: 01785 619131
E: sarah.elsom@btopenworld.co.uk
www.stafford.gov.uk

Curator: Sarah Elsom

The collection covers the history of this County Yeomanry Cavalry Regiment from its formation in 1794 to 1945. Special emphasis is laid on the World War II period where the Yeomanry fought at El Alamein and later took part in the D Day landings and the crossing of the Rhine (in swimming tanks). There is also an excellent collection of Victorian uniforms as well as items from the South African War and World War I. Throughout there are displays of weapons, medals, pictures, detailed models and audio-visual displays. The museum is designed to appeal to the general public as well as military enthusiasts. Some archives are held on site but the majority are in the County Record Office some 500m away.

Opening Hours: Tue–Sat 10am–4pm. Closed Bank Holidays

Admission: Free

Facilities: Toilets, shop

Warwick

QUEEN'S OWN HUSSARS MUSEUM

Located in the medieval Lord Leycester Hospital near the city centre. A 15-minute walk from the railway station and close to the bus station

The Queen's Own Hussars Museum,
Lord Leycester Hospital, 60 High Street,
Warwick CV34 4BH
T: and / F: 01926 492035
E: qohmuseum@qrh.org.uk
www.qohmuseum.org.uk

Queen's Own Hussars, 3rd King's Own Hussars, 3rd King's Own Light Dragoons, 3rd King's Own Regiment of Dragoons, 3rd Regiment of Dragoons, Leveson's Dragoons, Queen Consort's Own Regiment of Dragoons, 7th Queen's Own Hussars, 7th (Queen's Own) Regiment of Hussars, 7th (Queen's Own) Light Dragoons, 7th Queen's Own Regiment of Dragoons, Queen's Own Royal Regiment of Dragoons, Princess of Wales's Own Royal Regiment of Dragoons, Kerr's Dragoons, Polwarth's Dragoons, Jedburgh's Dragoons, Cunningham's Dragoons

This comprehensive collection covers the history of the Regiment from its foundation in the late 17th century, with emphasis on both horse and tank warfare. Key events in the Regiment's history, from the early battles of Dettingen and Waterloo onwards, are vividly recreated through the personal stories of individuals and a mixture of artefacts, equipment, documentation and weapons. New displays employ computer technology to illustrate the change-over from horses to tanks, the Regiment's decisive role at the Battle of El Alamein in World War II and its global peace-keeping role to the present. Interactive displays include a state-of-the-art reconstruction of an Afrika Korps Observation Post and events at El Alamein. There are artefacts and uniforms for handling and dressing up as well as more educational material in family packs for children and adults.

The Regimental archives of the 3rd and the 7th Hussars are held on site and may be viewed by appointment.

The admission charge of £4.90 also includes entry to the Hospital. Entry to the museum alone costs £2.50. Ex-Regimental Members can visit free of charge.

Opening Hours: Tue–Sat 10am–5pm (Summer) or 10am–4pm (Winter). Please call in advance to confirm current opening times

Admission: Entry to the Lord Leycester Hospital: Adults £4.90, Concessions £4.40, Children £3.90

Facilities: Parking, toilets, restaurant, shop, limited disabled access, research facilities

THE ROYAL REGIMENT OF FUSILIERS (ROYAL WARWICKSHIRE) MUSEUM

A short distance east of the city centre. Well signposted

The Royal Regiment of Fusiliers (Royal Warwickshire) Museum,
St John's House, Warwick CV34 4NF
T: 01926 491653 / F: 01869 497707
E: rrfwarksmuseum@btconnect.com
www.warwickfusiliers.co.uk

Curator: Major John Turquand

The Royal Regiment of Fusiliers, The Royal Warwickshire Fusiliers, The Royal Warwickshire Regiment, 6th (The Royal 1st Warwickshire) Regiment of Foot, 6th (or 1st Warwickshire) Regiment of Foot, 6th Regiment of Foot, Colonel Lillington's Regiment of Foot

The museum tells the story of the 6th Foot (Royal Warwickshire Regiment) from its raising in 1674 to The Royal Regiment of Fusiliers today. The story of the 'Warwickshire Lads', from Private to Field Marshal, is illustrated with an exciting collection of uniforms, weapons, equipment, badges, medals, pictures, documents and regimental memorabilia. The regimental library and archive are on site and may be viewed by appointment.

If travelling any distance to the museum please telephone in advance of your intended visit as staff shortage can very occasionally cause short notice closures.

Facebook page: Royal Regiment of Fusiliers Museum Royal Warwickshire)

Opening Hours: 10am–5pm Tue–Sat and Bank Holidays. Apr–Sep: Sun 2.30pm–5pm

Admission: Free

Facilities: Parking, toilets, shop. No wheelchair access to first floor

WARWICKSHIRE YEOMANRY MUSEUM

Near town centre, opposite Church Road

Warwickshire Yeomanry Museum,
The Court House, Jury Street,
Warwick CV34 4EW
T: 01926 492212
E: wtc.admin@btclick.com
www.warwickshire-yeomanry-museum.co.uk

Curator: BW Johnson

The museum covers the history of the Warwickshire Yeomanry from 1794 to 1956 with a collection of uniforms, weapons, medals and memorabilia. The Warwickshire Yeomanry together with the Queen's Own Worcestershire Hussars (Worcestershire Yeomanry) took part in the Affair of Huj on 8th November 1917 – the last classic unsupported Cavalry Charge of the Great War in Palestine immortalised by Lady Butler's painting which is on display in the museum. One of the 75mm Krupps Guns captured that day is also displayed in the museum. The regimental library and archive are held on site and may be viewed by appointment.

Opening Hours: Easter–Oct, Sat and Sun and Bank Holidays 10am–1pm and 2pm–4pm or at other times by appointment

Admission: Free

Facilities: Adjacent parking, shop

Worcester

WORCESTERSHIRE REGIMENT MUSEUM

Close to city centre at north end of the High Street

Worcestershire Regiment Museum Collection, City Museum and Art Gallery, Foregate Street, Worcester WR1 1DT
T: 01905 354359 / F: 01905 353871
E: museummercian@btconnect.com
www.wfrmuseum.org.uk

Curator: Major RS Prophet

Worcestershire and Sherwood Foresters Regiment, Worcestershire Regiment, 29th (or Worcestershire) Regiment of Foot, 29th Regiment of Foot, Colonel Farrington's Regiment of Foot, 36th (or Herefordshire) Regiment of Foot, 36th Regiment of Foot, Viscount Charlemont's Regiment of Foot, Worcestershire Yeomanry, Worcestershire Artillery, Militia and Volunteer units of the Worcestershire Regiment

This well presented collection covers the history of The Regiment from its raising in 1694 and that of The Worcestershire and Sherwood Foresters Regiment from 1970 to the present day with displays of uniforms, weapons, badges, medals and regimental memorabilia. The Regimental library and archive are not on site and research inquiries should be addressed to RHQ Mercian (Worcester), Norton Barracks, Worcester WR5 2PA or via the website address shown above. Please note that a fee of £15 (non refundable) will be charged for research inquiries

Opening Hours: Tues–Sat 10.30am–4.30pm

Admission: Free. Groups and school parties by appointment

Facilities: Toilets, refreshments, shop, disabled access. Parking nearby

WORCESTERSHIRE YEOMANRY MUSEUM COLLECTION

T: 01905 25371 / F: 01905 616979
E: artgalleryandmuseum@cityofworcester.gov.uk
www.worcestercitymuseum.org.uk

Curatorial Advisor: Philippa Tynsley

In the same building is the Worcestershire Yeomanry Museum Collection which covers the history of the County's Yeomanry Cavalry from 1794 up to its amalgamation with the Warwickshire Yeomanry in 1956.

East Midlands

Derby:	81	9th/12th Royal Lancers and Derbyshire Yeomanry Museum
Leicester:	82	Royal Leicestershire Regiment Museum
Lincoln:	83	Royal Lincolnshire Regiment and Lincolnshire Yeomanry Collections
Loughborough:	84	Leicestershire Yeomanry Museum Collection
Newark:	85	Queen's Royal Lancers Museum
Northampton:	86	Northamptonshire Regiment and Northamptonshire Yeomanry Collections
Nottingham:	87	South Nottinghamshire Hussars Yeomanry Museum
	88	The Sherwood Foresters (Notts and Derby Regiment) Collection
	89	Sherwood Rangers Yeomanry Museum

Derby

9TH/12TH ROYAL LANCERS

and

DERBYSHIRE YEOMANRY MUSEUM

Close to the city centre and attached to the city library

9th/12th Royal Lancers Museum, Derby Museum and Art Gallery, The Strand, Derby, Derbyshire DE1 1BS
T: 01332 641913 / F: 01332 716670
E: Mike.Galer@derby.gov.uk
www.derby.gov.uk/museums

Curator: Dr Mike Galer

9th/12th Royal Lancers (Prince of Wales's Own), 9th Queen's Royal Lancers, 9th (Queen's) Lancers, 9th Light Dragoons, 9th Dragoons, Wynne's Dragoons, 12th Royal Lancers (Prince of Wales's), 12th (Prince of Wales's Royal) Lancers, 12th (Prince of Wales's) Light Dragoons, 12th Dragoons, Bowle's Dragoons, Derbyshire Yeomanry

The Regimental Museum Display is housed within the Soldier's Story gallery at Derby Museum

Soldier's Story
The military gallery at Derby Museum was re-furbished 2006–8 with the aid of a grant from the Heritage Lottery Fund (HLF), in partnership with the 9th/12th Lancers, the Derbyshire Yeomanry, Worcestershire and Sherwood Foresters Regiment and Derby City Council. The new gallery opened on 25 October 2008.

New high-specification cases have been installed, along with new high-technology fixtures and fittings and stunning graphics. There are over 200 objects that have never been seen before by the public, including weapons, medals, uniforms, personal equipment, navigation and communication equipment, food and other items. There are two database units to explore our archive material, films and stories of soldiers as well as a mock-up of a tank turret and a small slice of a World War I trench with sound-effects for both and a large video wall. Highlights include Victoria Crosses, on display for the first time, and a full-size reconstruction of a World War I-era Lancer on horseback with full equipment.

The 9th/12th Royal Lancers
The museum traces the history of the 9th Lancers, 12th Lancers and since 1960 the 9th/12th Lancers, through its displays of uniforms, medals, weapons and lances, sporting equipment, and personal items alongside that of material associated with the Sherwood Foresters and the Derbyshire Yeomanry. A touch-screen computer in the gallery provides access to the museum's archive of men who served in World War I, 1914–19, in particular but also soldiers from the 1820s to the present day. The touch-screen is based on the Museum's digitised archive and represents only a

small portion of the data that may be available. The material available in the gallery is strong on the Boer War and World War I and weaker for more modern periods.

Derbyshire Yeomanry and The Sherwood Foresters
In addition to the material of the 9th/12th Lancers, the Museum also has displays covering the Derbyshire Yeomanry and the Derby/Derbyshire elements of the Worcestershire and Sherwood Foresters Regiment, including the Derby Militias and the 95th Regiment of Foot. These are integrated with the Lancers displays in Soldier's Story.

Opening Hours: Mon 11am–5pm, Tue–Sat 10am–5pm, Sun and Bank Holidays 1pm–4pm

Admission: Free

Facilities: Toilets, shop, disabled access. Nearby parking and cafés

Leicester

ROYAL LEICESTERSHIRE REGIMENT MUSEUM

West of the main shopping area and east of the river, the museum is easily accessible by foot from the city centre

Royal Leicestershire Regiment Museum Collection,
Newarke Houses Museum, The Newarke, Leicester LE2 7BY
T: 0116 2254980 / F: 0116 2254982
E: museums@leicester.gov.uk
www.leicester.gov.uk/museums

Curator: Philip French

Royal Leicestershire Regiment, Leicestershire Regiment, 17th (or Leicestershire) Regiment of Foot, 17th Regiment of Foot, Colonel Richard's Regiment of Foot

The regimental collection has recently moved into dedicated galleries in the refurbished Newarke Houses Museum. It illustrates the history of the Regiment from 1688 to 1964 when it became part of what is now the Royal Anglian Regiment. Displays include uniforms, medals, regimental memorabilia, photographs, video and interactive family history. They address topics such as recruiting and army life. A touch screen computer is available in the gallery for ancestor research.

Opening Hours: Mon–Sat 10am–5pm, Sun 11am–5pm. Closed Dec 24, 25, 26 and 31, and Jan 1

Admission: Free

Facilities: Parking, toilets, refreshments, disabled access

Lincoln

ROYAL LINCOLNSHIRE REGIMENT

and

LINCOLNSHIRE YEOMANRY COLLECTIONS

Located on the B1398, 0.5 miles northwest of the Cathedral. City Bus no 1

Royal Lincolnshire Regiment Museum Collection, Museum of Lincoln Life, Burton Road, Lincoln LN1 3LY
T: 01522 521754 / F: 01522 537354
E: Caroline.Frisby@lincolnshire.gov.uk
www.lincolnshire.gov.uk

Collections Officer (Regimental):
Caroline Frisby

Royal Anglian Regiment, Royal Lincolnshire Regiment, Lincolnshire Regiment, 10th (or North Lincolnshire) Regiment of Foot, 10th Regiment of Foot, Earl of Bath's Regiment of Foot, Lincolnshire Yeomanry

The Collections of the Royal Lincolnshire Regiment and the Lincolnshire Yeomanry, now in the care of Lincolnshire County Council, are housed in a listed barracks which was built in 1857 for the Royal Lincoln Militia. The displays of uniforms, weapons, badges, medals and regimental memorabilia cover the history of the County Infantry Regiment from 1685 onwards. Exhibits illustrate the Regiment's service in the American War of Independence, the Sudan campaign, the Boer War and both world wars. A separate display is devoted to uniforms, medals and photographs of the Lincolnshire Yeomanry.

Please note that the archive material of the Royal Lincolnshire Regiment is now located at Lincolnshire Archives.

Opening Hours: Summer, 10am–4pm daily. Winter (Oct–Mar) 10am–4pm Mon–Sat. Last admissions 3.15pm.

Admission: Free. Groups and school parties by appointment.

Facilities: Parking, toilets, tearoom, shop, disabled access, audio guide

Loughborough

LEICESTERSHIRE YEOMANRY MUSEUM COLLECTION

Town centre location

Leicestershire Yeomanry Museum Collection, Carillon and Tower Museum, Queen's Park, Loughborough, Leicestershire LE11 3DU
T: 01509 231667 / F: 01509 634839
E: carillonmuseum@talktalk.net

Archivist: Pauline Cutter

The Leicestershire Yeomanry Collection is displayed on the first floor of this museum which otherwise contains objects from a number of British and Allied World War II units of all three services. Postal enquiries should be addressed to the Chairman of the Trust, Mr Peter Crooks, c/o John Storer House, Wards End, Loughborough, Leicestershire LE11 2HA

Opening Hours: Good Fri to 30 Sep, 1pm–4.30pm, Tues–Sun. Closed Bank Holidays

Admission: Adults 50p, Seniors and Children free

Facilities: Café and toilets nearby (150m), shop, partial wheelchair access. Disabled parking and drop-off point

E. MIDLANDS

Newark

QUEEN'S ROYAL LANCERS MUSEUM

The Queen's Royal Lancers Museum is re-locating to Thoresby Courtyard, Thoresby Park, Thoresby, Newark, NG22 9ER in 2011. For information about the move and new location contact:

Home Headquarters, The Queen's Royal Lancers, Lancer House, Prince William of Gloucester Barracks, Grantham, Lincolnshire NG31 7TJ
T: 0115 9573295
E: qrlmuseum@btinternet.com
www.qrlassociation.co.uk

Curator: Captain JM Holtby
Assistant curator: Robert Osborn

The Queen's Royal Lancers, 16th/5th Queen's Royal Lancers, 16th Queen's Lancers, 16th (Queen's) Light Dragoons, 16th Light Dragoons (Burgoyne's Light Horse), 5th Royal Irish Lancers, 5th (Royal Irish) Lancers, 5th (Royal Irish) Dragoons, 17th/21st Lancers, 17th (Duke of Cambridge's Own) Lancers, 17th Lancers, 17th Light Dragoons, 21st (Empress of India's) Lancers, 21st Hussars, 21st Light Dragoons, Bengal European Cavalry (Honourable East India Company)

The Queen's Royal Lancers Museum is currently in storage pending relocation to Thoresby Park in Spring 2011. The new museum will include representative displays from the South Nottinghamshire Hussars Yeomanry and the Sherwood Rangers Yeomanry. For further information contact the curator or visit the Regimental website. For historical enquiries contact the curator on the above telephone number or email.

The regimental collections of the Queen's Royal Lancers and its immediate antecedent regiments the 16th/5th Lancers and the 17th/21st Lancers, currently held in storage at Prince William of Gloucester Barracks, Grantham, include fine displays of uniforms, weapons, medals, badges, silver and paintings tracing the regiments' history from Marlborough's campaign to the Gulf War. The Regimental archive is held at Lancer House, Grantham, and may be viewed by appointment.

Details of opening time, admission charges and facilities will be available on the museum website or from the address shown above.

Northampton

NORTHAMPTONSHIRE REGIMENT

and

NORTHAMPTONSHIRE YEOMANRY COLLECTIONS

On the outskirts of town, off the A4500 Wellingborough Road

Northamptonshire Regiment and Northamptonshire Yeomanry Collections, Abington Museum, Abington Park, Northampton NN1 5LW
T: 01604 838111 / F: 01604 830720
E: abingtonmuseum@northampton.gov.uk
www.northampton.gov.uk/museums

Cultural Development Team Leader: Peter Field

Royal Anglian Regiment, Northamptonshire Regiment, 48th (or the Northamptonshire) Regiment of Foot, 48th Regiment of Foot, Colonel Cholmondley's Regiment of Foot, 58th (or the Rutlandshire) Regiment of Foot, 58th Regiment of Foot raised by Colonel Robert Anstruther as 60th Foot, Northamptonshire Yeomanry

The Regimental Collection traces the history of the County Regiment from its formation in 1741 up to its amalgamation in 1960. Items include uniforms, prints, pictures, silver, medals and other items of Regimental significance. Uniforms and medals form the core of the Yeomanry Collection. Regimental archives are held at the Northamptonshire Record Office.

Opening Hours: Open: Apr–Oct, Thurs–Sun 1pm–5pm, Bank Holiday Mondays 1pm–5pm. Closed Nov–Mar

Admission: Free

Facilities: Toilets, disabled toilet and access to ground floor, baby changing facilities. Parking nearby

Nottingham

SOUTH NOTTINGHAMSHIRE HUSSARS YEOMANRY MUSEUM

South Nottinghamshire Hussars Yeomanry Museum,
The TA Centre, Hucknall Lane, Bulwell,
Nottingham NG6 8AQ
T: 0115 9272251
E: 100RA-307-AO@mod.uk

Curator: Gil Aldridge

A small regimental collection which is open to the public by appointment only.

The regiment will also contribute a representative display to the new Queen's Royal Lancers and Nottinghamshire Yeomanry Museum which is being established at Thoresby Park in Spring 2011. *See p66* **85**

THE SHERWOOD FORESTERS (NOTTS AND DERBY REGIMENT) COLLECTION

Close to the city centre and railway station

The Sherwood Foresters (Notts and Derby Regiment) Collection, The Castle,
Nottingham NG1 6EL
T: 0115 9465415 / F: 0115 9469853
E: rhqmercian.notts@btconnect.com
www.wfrmuseum.org.uk

Curator: Lt Col K Seddon

2nd Battalion The Mercian Regiment (Worcesters and Foresters), The Worcestershire & Sherwood Foresters Regiment (29th/45th Foot), Sherwood Foresters (Nottinghamshire & Derbyshire Regiment), Sherwood Foresters (Derbyshire Regiment), Derbyshire Regiment (Sherwood Foresters), 45th (Nottinghamshire)Regiment, Sherwood Foresters, 45th (1st Nottinghamshire) Regiment, Robin Hood Volunteer Rifles, 45th Regiment of Foot, 95th (Derbyshire) Regiment of Foot, 95th Regiment of Foot

Displays cover the history of the Regiment from 1741 through its amalgamation with the Worcestershire Regiment in 1970 to become The Worcestershire and Sherwood Foresters Regiment and to the amalgamation with the Cheshire and Staffordshire Regiments to form the Mercian Regiment. Objects on display include many of the Regiment's Colours, uniforms, headdress, badges and medals. Within the Gallery is a touch screen with details of many Sherwood Foresters (some with photographs) from 1741 to 1970. The Archives (with a database of over 95 thousand soldiers) are held separately at Foresters House, Chetwynd Barracks, Chilwell and are accessible by appointment only on Tel: 0115.9465415. Written and telephone enquiries are welcomed and enquiries can also be submitted from our website. The Museum offers an educational outreach programme to both Primary and Secondary schools, Higher Education Faculties and Community Groups. Further details can be found on our website.

There is also a display in Derby City Museum and Art Gallery shared with the 9th/12th Royal Lancers and the Derbyshire Yeomanry.

Opening Hours: Mar–Sep: daily 10am–5pm. Oct–Feb: daily 11am–4pm. Closed Christmas Day, Boxing Day and New Year's Day

Admission: Adults £3, concessions and Children £1.50

Facilities: Toilets, refreshments, shop, disabled access

SHERWOOD RANGERS YEOMANRY MUSEUM

East of Nottingham just off the B686

Sherwood Rangers Yeomanry Museum,
S (SRY) Sqn The Royal Yeomanry, Cavendish Drive, Carlton, Nottinghamshire NG4 3DX
T: 0115 9618722
E: info@thesherwoodrangers.org
www.sherwoodrangers.com

A small regimental collection which is open to the public by appointment only. Contact should be made through the Chairman of the Old Comrades Association, Mr M. Freeman, who can be contacted at the e-mail and website addresses shown above.

The Regiment will also contribute a representative display to the new Queen's Royal Lancers and Nottinghamshire Yeomanry Museum which is being established at Thoresby Park in Spring 2011. *See p66* **85**

E. MIDLANDS

North West

Carlisle 92

98

Isle of Man 94

95

99 100

91

Manchester 90

Liverpool
96 97

93

NORTH WEST

Ashton-under-Lyne:	90	Manchester Regiment
Bury:	91	The Fusilier Museum
Carlisle:	92	Border regiment and King's Own Royal Border Regiment
Chester:	93	Cheshire Military Museum
Isle of Man:	94	Museum of the Manx Regiment
Lancaster:	95	King's Own Royal Regiment
Liverpool:	96	King's Regiment
	97	Liverpool Scottish Regiment
Penrith:	98	Westmorland and Cumberland Yeomanry
Preston:	99	14th / 20th King's Hussars and Duke of Lancaster's Own Yeomanry
	100	Queen's Lancashire Regiment

Ashton-under-Lyne

MANCHESTER REGIMENT MUSEUM 90

In the town centre near railway and bus stations and car park

Manchester Regiment Museum,
Town Hall, Market Place,
Ashton-under-Lyne, Tameside OL6 6DL
T: 0161 3422254 / F: 0161 3432869
E: garry.smith1@tameside.gov.uk
www.tameside.gov.uk/
museumsgalleries/mom

Curator: Garry Smith

Manchester Regiment, 63rd (or the West Suffolk) Regiment of Foot, 63rd Regiment of Foot (Colonel Robert Armiger), 2nd Bn of the 8th (The King's) Regiment of Foot, 96th Regiment of Foot, 96th (Queen's Own) Regiment of Foot, 96th Regiment of Foot (raised as 2nd Bn 52nd Foot), 96th (The Queen's Royal Irish) Regiment, 96th(British Musketeers) Regiment, 96th Regiment of Foot, 97th (Queen's German) Regiment of Foot, 97th (Queen's Own Royal) Regiment of Foot, 104th (Royal Manchester Volunteers), Lancashire Rifle Volunteer Corps. Small collections for the King's Regiment and Duke of Lancaster's Regiment with Tameside focus.

The Museum tells the story of generations of soldiers, from the raising of the Regiment in 1756 through to Regimental life today. The Museum's Ladysmith Gallery (re-developed in 2002) tells our story chronologically, covering major actions such as the American War of Independence, New Zealand, the Crimea, South Africa, both world wars and the Malayan Emergency. The Gallery also houses over 1,800 medals, including six Victoria Cross Groups as well as a reconstruction of a World War I trench. The Forshaw Gallery (re-developed in 2006) covers themed aspects of our story including recreation, daily routine, the soldier as collector, Regimental insignia, Regimental dress, mess life and some of our Regimental Treasures. The Gallery also includes a reconstruction of a Barrack Room from Ladysmith Barracks and an original Army Jeep, as well as many family-friendly interactives that bring our story to life for the whole family. The Special Exhibition space changes every six months. This space highlights the lesser-known aspects of our history and gives repeat visitors something new to see each time they visit.

The Regimental Archives are deposited with Tameside Local Studies and Archives Centre, just 10 minutes walk from the Museum. Here they are publicly accessible, without charge, six days a week. For more information please contact the Archive Centre directly on 0161 342 4242.

Opening Hours: Mon–Sat 10am–4pm

Admission: Free. Groups and school parties by appointment

Facilities: Toilets, shop, lecture room, disabled access. Adjacent parking

Bury

THE FUSILIER MUSEUM 91

Town centre location

The Fusilier Museum, Moss Street,
Bury, BL9 0DF
T: 0161 763 8950
E: enquiries@fusiliermuseum.com
www.fusiliermuseum.com

Curator: Lt Col Mike Glover

Royal Regiment of Fusiliers, Lancashire Fusiliers, 20th (or East Devonshire) Regiment of Foot, 20th Regiment of Foot, Colonel Sir Robert Peyton's Companies of Foot

The Fusilier Museum in Bury tells the exciting story of one of Lancashire's most famous Regiments. The Regiment of six VCs before breakfast at Gallipoli, indeed the regiment that earned more VCs in World War I than any other infantry regiment in the British Army. The archive and displays illustrate the stories of famous members of the Regiment from Wolfe storming Quebec and Ross burning the White House, to the Regiment's connection with Napoleon and Tolkein and the creation of Lord of the Rings. The regimental library and archive are on site and may be viewed by appointment. The museum has moved from Wellington Barracks to the centre of Bury, and opened on 27th June 2009. The museum has a new collection, that of the Royal Regiment of Fusiliers. Although the Regiment was formed in 1968, this is the first time the Regiment has had its own museum and place to commemorate its history – from the streets of Northern Ireland to Afghanistan, the Regiment's most recent operational deployment.

Opening Hours: 10am–4pm daily

Admission: Adults £2, Seniors £1, Children £1. Groups and school parties by appointment

Facilities: Parking, toilets, shop, lecture room

NORTH WEST

Carlisle

BORDER REGIMENT AND KING'S OWN ROYAL BORDER REGIMENT MUSEUM

North side of city centre, a 15-minute walk from station. By car, exit M6 at J43 or 44

Border Regiment and King's Own Royal Border Regiment Museum, Queen Mary's Tower, The Castle, Carlisle, Cumbria CA3 8UR
T: 01228 532774 / F: 01228 545435
E: borderregiment@aol.com and korbrmuseum@aol.com
www.kingsownbordermuseum.btik.com

Curator: Stuart Eastwood
Assistant Curator: Tony Goddard

Duke of Lancaster's Regiment (King's, Lancashire and Border), King's Own Royal Border Regiment, Border Regiment, 34th (Cumberland) Regiment of Foot, 34th Regiment of Foot, Lord Lucas's Regiment of Foot, 55th (Westmoreland) Regiment of Foot, 55th Regiment of Foot, 57th Regiment of Foot (Colonel George Perry), Royal Cumberland Militia, Cumberland Militia, Royal Westmorland Light Infantry Militia, Westmorland Militia, Cumberland and Westmorland Rifle Volunteers, Cumberland Artillery

Located within the Inner Ward of Carlisle Castle, the Museum relates the history of Cumbria's County Infantry Regiment, the Border Regiment (34th and 55th Foot) and its successor The King's Own Royal Border Regiment, local militia, volunteer and Territorial Army units from 1702 to the present day. Wide-ranging displays on two floors include uniforms, weapons, equipment, medals, silver, pictures, memorabilia, and a recreated Word War I trench and other dioramas. The Castle, founded in 1092, is a superb medieval fortress owned by the Crown and maintained by English Heritage. It can boast almost continuous military occupation for 900 years and preserved within its walls are the 19th-century barracks and military buildings used by The Border Regimental Depot from 1873 to 1959.

The Museum has extensive archives. Family history and other enquiries are welcome, personal callers preferably by appointment. For detailed research a minimum donation will be sought.

Opening Hours: Apr–Sep: 9.30am–5pm daily. Nov–Mar: 10am–4pm daily. Closed 24–26 Dec and 1 Jan

Admission: Included in entry charge to Castle: Adults £4.80, Concessions £4.10, Children (under 16) £2.40

Facilities: Research service with access to the regimental archives available by appointment. Education Service provided. Guided tours by arrangement. Toilets (including disabled), lecture room, shop, disabled access to ground floor, picnic area, disabled parking at the Castle, other parking nearby

Chester

CHESHIRE MILITARY MUSEUM

Follow signs to the castle from city centre

Cheshire Military Museum, The Castle, Chester, Cheshire CH1 2DN
T: 01244 327617 / F: 01244 401700
E: cheshiremilitarymuseum@live.co.uk
www.cheshiremilitarymuseum.co.uk

Curator: Major Eddie Pickering

22nd (Cheshire) Regiment (The 1st Battalion the Mercian Regiment (Cheshire)), Cheshire Regiment (22nd Foot), 22nd (or the Cheshire) Regiment of Foot, 22nd Regiment of Foot, Duke of Norfolk's Regiment of Foot, Cheshire Yeomanry. Representative collections of 3rd Carabiniers, 5th Inniskilling Dragoon Guards and Eaton Hall Officer Cadet School

An innovative and attractive museum relating the story of the men of the regiments of Cheshire, their families and their community. This 300 year history is told through art, artefacts and memorabilia including fine displays of uniforms, medals and weapons. The War Horse exhibition traces the story of the horse and other equine beasts in war from the times of the Ancient Egyptians to the modern day.

Details of this and other museum displays can be seen on the website. Access to the archives is available by appointment.

Opening Hours: Daily 10am–5pm (last admission 4pm). Closed for two weeks over Christmas and New Year

Admission: Adults £3, Seniors and Children £2. Groups and school parties by appointment

Facilities: Shop and disabled access. Adjacent toilets and parking

Isle of Man

MUSEUM OF THE MANX REGIMENT

To the south of the airport terminal on the road between Ballasalla and Castletown

Museum of the Manx Regiment,
Ronaldsway Airport, Ballasalla,
Isle of Man IM2 2AT
T: 01624 829294
E: iramsden@talk21.com
www.maps.iofm.net/museum

Director: Ivor Ramsden

15th (I.O.M.) Light A.A., Regiment, R.A. (T.A.)

Now re-designed and collocated with the Manx Aviation and Military Museum at the Island's airport, the Manx Regiment Museum commemorates the part played by the Island's Regiment during World War II both in the defence of the Isle of Man itself and in overseas theatres such as Egypt, Eritrea, Crete, Italy, France, Holland and Germany. The collection is rich in Regimental memorabilia and includes a 40mm Bofors anti-aircraft gun on a towed mounting and a very rare 1944 Morris-Commercial C9/B self-propelled Bofors gun as used by the Regiment in north west Europe.

Opening Hours: Sat, Sun and Bank Holidays 10am–4.30pm.

Admission: Free. Groups and school parties by appointment

Facilities: Parking, toilets, shop, disabled access

Lancaster

KING'S OWN ROYAL REGIMENT

Located in pedestrian City centre a 5-minute walk from railway station. By road: A6, M6 (J33 South or J34 North)

King's Own Royal Regiment Museum,
City Museum, Market Square, Lancaster,
Lancashire LA1 1HT
T: 01524 555619 or 01524 64637
F: 01524 841692
E: kingsownmuseum@iname.com
www.kingsownmuseum.plus.co.uk

Curator: Peter Donnelly

King's Own Royal Border Regiment, King's Own (Royal Lancaster) Regiment, King's Own Royal Regiment (Lancaster), King's Own (Royal Lancaster) Regiment, 4th (The King's Own Royal) Regiment of Foot, 4th (or King's Own) Regiment of Foot, King's Own Regiment of Foot, Queen's Marines, Queen's Own Regiment of Foot, Queen Consort's Regiment, Queen's Regiment, Duchess of York and Albany's Regiment, Earl of Plymouth's Regiment for Tangier (2nd Tangier Regiment), 1st Royal Lancashire Militia.

The museum, housed in the old Town Hall of 1783, was the first municipal museum to include a regimental museum. It tells the story of the King's Own Royal Regiment from 1680 to the present day. Topics covered include the Napoleonic campaigns, the Crimean War, the expedition to Abyssinia, both world wars and subsequent operations and events in which the regiment has participated. Displays include a social history of soldiers who served in the Regiment. There is extensive archive material which is accessible by appointment.

Opening Hours: Mon–Sat 10am–5pm. Closed Christmas and New Year

Admission: Free. Groups and school parties by appointment

Facilities: Parking, shop, lecture room

NORTH WEST

Liverpool

KING'S REGIMENT MUSEUM

In the Museum of Liverpool at the Pier Head

King's Regiment Museum Collection,
Dock Traffic Office, Pier Head,
Liverpool L3 4AX
T: 0151 478 4065 / F: 0151 478 4090
E: karen.orourke@liverpoolmuseums.org.uk
www.army.mod.uk/lancs

Curator: Karen O'Rourke

King's Regiment (Manchester and Liverpool), King's Regiment (Liverpool), King's (Liverpool Regiment), 8th (or the King's) Regiment of Foot, King's Regiment of Foot, Queen's Regiment of Foot (or Webb's Regiment), Princess Anne of Denmark's Regiment of Foot

The Museum of Liverpool Life and the King's Regiment Museum closed on 4 June 2006. The new Museum of Liverpool opens at the Pier Head, Liverpool in 2011. It will feature the King's Regiment collection and a World War I experience gallery. Archive inquiries should be sent to the Regimental Headquarters at citysecliv@lancs.army.mod.uk

LIVERPOOL SCOTTISH REGIMENTAL MUSEUM **97**

1 mile east of city centre. Off B5178 near Wavertree Park

Contact address:
Major IL Riley, 51a Common Lane,
Culcheth, Warrington WA3 4EY
T: 01925 766157 or 0151 645 5717 or
07952.2169285
E: ilriley@liverpoolscottish.org.uk
www.liverpoolscottish.org.uk

Hon. Secretary: Major IL Riley

19th Lancashire Rifle Volunteers (Liverpool Lowland Volunteers), 71st Lancashire Rifle Volunteers (Liverpool Highland Volunteers), 8th (Scottish) Volunteer Bn King's Liverpool Regiment, 10th (Scottish) Bn King's (Liverpool Regiment TF), 1st and 2nd Bns The Liverpool Scottish Queen's Own Cameron Highlanders, 89th Anti-Tank Regiment Royal Artillery, 655th Light Anti-Aircraft Regiment Royal Artillery, 'V' (The Liverpool Scottish) Company 1st Bn Highland Volunteers, 'V' (Liverpool Scottish) Company 5th/8th(Volunteer) Bn, The King's Regiment and successor sub-units in the King's and Cheshire Regiment and the Duke of Lancaster's Regiment

This rich collection of regimental artefacts that offers a comprehensive representation of the life of a Territorial infantry battalion over the last hundred years is currently in store pending re-location. The regimental museum is therefore closed but access to extensive archive material is available at New Zealand House in Liverpool through the contacts shown above. The archives include diaries, scrapbooks and records of a significant number of soldiers who have served with the regiment together with a database of soldiers who served and also of all Merseyside War Memorials.

Admission to the archives: Normally Wednesdays 10.30am–3pm in Liverpool (appointment advised) and other times by arrangement.

Facilities: Toilets

Penrith

WESTMORLAND AND CUMBERLAND YEOMANRY MUSEUM

On the A592 Penrith to Ullswater road

Westmorland and Cumberland Yeomanry Museum, Dalemain Historic House and Gardens, near Penrith, Cumbria CA11 0HB
T: 01768 486450 / F: 01768 486223
E: admin@dalemain.com
www.dalemain.com

Curator: RB Hassell-McCosh

Located in the base of the Norman pele tower, the museum contains many mementoes and relics of the Westmorland and Cumberland Yeomanry as well as the two volunteer forces that preceded it – the Westmorland East and West Wards Local Militia and Cumberland Loyal Leath Ward Volunteers. The displays trace the Regiment's history with particular reference to the Boer War and its role in the Great War as Divisional Cavalry with Kitchener's Army in France.

Opening Hours: Easter–Oct: Sun–Thu 11.15am–4pm (3pm in Oct)

Admission: Included in charge for entry to house and gardens. Adults £9, Seniors £8.50, accompanied Children (under 16) free. Groups and school parties by appointment

Facilities: Parking, toilets, shop

Preston

14TH/20TH KING'S HUSSARS MUSEUM COLLECTION

and

DUKE OF LANCASTER'S OWN YEOMANRY MUSEUM COLLECTION

Within 400 yards of the bus station on ring road near the junction with Church Street

Museum of Lancashire, Stanley Street, Preston, Lancashire PR1 4YP
T: 01772 264075
www.lancashire.gov.uk

Curator: Dr Stephen Bull

King's Royal Hussars, 14th/20th King's Hussars, 14th (King's) Hussars, 14th (King's) Light Dragoons, 14th (Duchess of York's Own) Light Dragoons, 14th Light Dragoons, 14th Dragoons, 14th Hussars, 20th Hussars, 2nd Bengal European Light Cavalry (Honourable East India Company), Duke of Lancaster's Own Yeomanry, Representative collections of Lancashire Regiments, Loan collection of Queen's Lancashire Regiment

Due to re-open in mid 2011 following a major refit, the Museum of Lancashire contains the museums of two historic regiments. The gallery of the 14th/20th King's Hussars traces the history of the Regiment from 1715 and includes two Victoria crosses as well as artefacts from the Napoleonic era and India. The Duke of Lancaster's Own Yeomanry collection marks its association with the county with exhibits that include items from World War I in the Middle East, Peterloo, and South Africa. Mounted in co-operation with the Duke of Lancaster's Regiment and Lancashire Fusiliers, a new area follows Lancastrians in World War I, and includes a trench scene with many of the devices of trench warfare as well as Imperial War Museum film footage. There is also a display on the Home Front in Lancashire during World War II.

Opening hours: 10.30am–5pm. Closed Thu, Sun and Bank Holidays

Admission: Adults £3, concessions £2, accompanied children free. Groups and school parties by appointment

Facilities: Parking, toilets, refreshments, shop, disabled access, lecture room

North-east of town centre on B6245

Queen's Lancashire Regiment Museum,
Fulwood Barracks, Watling Street Road,
Preston, Lancashire PR2 8AA
T: 01772 260362 / F: 01772 260583
E: qlrmuseum@btconnect.com
www.qlrmuseum.co.uk

Curator: Jane Davies

The Duke of Lancaster's Regiment, The Queen's Lancashire Regiment, The East Lancashire Regiment: 30th and 59th Foot, The South Lancashire Regiment (Prince of Wales's Volunteers): 40th and 82nd Foot, The Loyal Regiment (North Lancashire): 47th and 81st Foot, The Lancashire Regiment (Prince of Wales's Volunteers)

The museum houses the largest military collection in the North West. It covers the history of the County's three infantry regiments from the raising of Lord Castleton's Regiment of Foot in 1689 through the several amalgamations that have resulted in the creation of the current Duke of Lancaster's Regiment. Objects related to the County's Militia, Rifle Volunteers, Territorial Army, Home Guard and Cadet Units are also on display. The collection, archive and library hold extensive historical material including uniform, badges, medals, weapons and equipment as well as photographs, film and sound, ceramics and fine and decorative art.

Opening Hours: Tue–Thu 9am–4pm or by appointment. Sat 10am–4pm

Admission: Free. Groups and school parties by appointment

Facilities: Parking, toilets, shop, lecture room. Adjacent pubs/cafés

NORTH WEST

Yorkshire

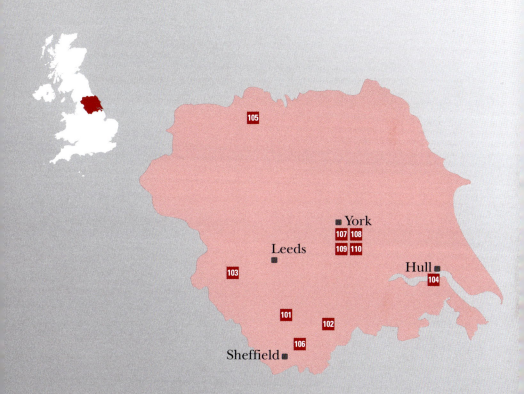

Barnsley:	101	13th/18th Royal Hussars and Light Dragoons
Doncaster:	102	King's Own Yorkshire Light Infantry
Halifax:	103	Duke of Wellington's Regiment
Hull:	104	4th Battalion East Yorkshire Regiment
Richmond:	105	Green Howards
Rotherham:	106	York and Lancaster Regiment
York:	107	Kohima Museum
	108	Prince of Wales's Own Regiment of Yorkshire
	109	Queen's Own Yorkshire Yeomanry
	110	Royal Dragoon Guards

Barnsley

13TH/18TH ROYAL HUSSARS (QUEEN MARY'S OWN)

and

THE LIGHT DRAGOONS MUSEUM

Bus 236 (Huddersfield), along A635 and A637 roads to Cawthorne and Kexbrough

13th/18th Royal Hussars (QMO) and Light Dragoons Museum, Cannon Hall, Cawthorne, Barnsley, South Yorkshire S75 4AT
T: 01226 790270 / F: 01226 792117
E: mail@lightdragoons.org.uk
www.lightdragoons.org.uk/
regimental_history/cannonhall.php

Curator: Captain GE Locker

The Light Dragoons, 13th/18th Royal Hussars, 13th Hussars, 13th Light Dragoons, 18th Royal Hussars (Queen Mary's Own), 18th Light Dragoons

The Collection covers the history of the 13th/18th Royal Hussars with a series of displays illustrating the life of the Regiment in peace and war from 1715 to the present time. Exhibits relate to the Battle of Waterloo, Charge of the Light Brigade, Boer War, both world wars and The Light Dragoons' involvement in recent UN and NATO operations.

Opening Hours: Apr–Oct, Sat–Wed 11am–5pm (last admission 4.15pm). Closed Thurs and Fri. Nov, Dec, Mar: Sun only 11am–4pm. Museum closed Jan and Feb.

Admission: Free

Facilities: Parking, toilets, refreshments, shop, lecture room, education service, corporate events

Doncaster

KING'S OWN YORKSHIRE LIGHT INFANTRY MUSEUM

Close to Doncaster town centre, off Waterdale

King's Own Yorkshire Light Infantry Museum, Doncaster Museum and Art Gallery, Chequer Road, Doncaster, South Yorkshire DN1 2AE
T: 01302 734293 / F: 01302 735409
E: museum@doncaster.gov.uk
www.doncaster.gov.uk/museums

Curator: Laura Nugent

King's Own Yorkshire Light Infantry, 51st (2nd Yorkshire West Riding), 105th (Madras Light Infantry)

The Regimental Gallery of the King's Own Yorkshire Light Infantry is located in the same building as Doncaster Museum and Art Gallery. The gallery displays an excellent collection of Regimental memorabilia, uniforms, pictures and silver dating from the raising of the Regiment in 1755 to its amalgamation into The Light Infantry in 1968. It includes a model of the Pontefract Barracks, the Roll of Honour of the 5th Battalion and one of the most extensive medal collections in this country. A list of the medals awarded to soldiers serving with the KOYLI which are held in the Regimental Museum at Doncaster Museum and Art Gallery is shown on the museum's website.

The museum is likely to be closed for refurbishment from July 2010 to March 2011. See website for details.

Although the KOYLI Gallery is housed in Doncaster Museum, enquiries relating to the archives of the Regiment should be addressed to:

The Regimental Secretary,
Light Infantry Office (Yorkshire),
Minden House,
Wakefield Road,
Pontefract, WF8 4ES.
Tel: 01977 703181, or email: yorkshire@the-rifles.co.uk

Opening Hours: Mon–Sat 10am–5pm

Admission: Free

Facilities: Parking, toilets, shop, full disabled access and adapted toilets

YORKSHIRE

Halifax

DUKE OF WELLINGTON'S REGIMENT (WEST RIDING) MUSEUM

1 mile from town centre on the A647 to Queensbury and Bradford

The Duke of Wellington's Regiment (West Riding) Museum, Bankfield Museum, Boothtown Road, Halifax, West Yorkshire HX3 6HG
T: 01422 354823/352334
F: 01422 349020
E: rhq@dukesrhq.demon.co.uk
www.dwr.org.uk

Curatorial Adviser: Franne Wills
Military Keeper: John Spencer

Duke of Wellington's (West Riding) Regiment, 33rd Duke of Wellington's Regiment, 33rd (or 1st Yorkshire West Riding) Regiment of Foot, 33rd Regiment of Foot, Earl of Huntingdon's Regiment of Foot, 76th Regiment of Foot, 76th (Hindoostan) Regiment of Foot

The Collection illustrates the history of the Regiment from the raising of the 33rd Foot in 1702 and the 76th Foot in 1787 to the present day. The Museum has undergone a recent redesign to tell the story of the Regiment through the eyes of the soldiers who served in it. Each period case focuses on two or three soldiers and tells their story in their own words through recordings and displays of their life in the Regiment. Other exhibits relate to the local Volunteer, Militia and Territorial Forces and there are displays of objects associated with the Iron Duke himself and the Regiment's heritage as a name synonymous with rugby in the British Army. Access to the Regimental archive is by appointment.

Opening Hours: Tue–Sat and Bank Holiday Mondays 10am–5pm, Sun 1pm–4pm. Closed Mondays (except Bank Holidays) Christmas Day, Boxing Day and New Year's Day

Admission: Free

Facilities: Free parking, toilets, shop, lecture room, disabled access

Hull

4TH BATTALION EAST YORKSHIRE REGIMENT COLLECTION

4th Bn East Yorkshire Regiment Collection, Wilberforce House Museum, 25 High Street, Kingston-upon-Hull HU1 1NQ
T: 01482 616431
E: vanessa.salter@hullcc.gov.uk

Curator: Vanessa Salter

The Collection, which also includes items from the East Yorks Militia and Rifle Volunteers, is temporarily being held in store but may be viewed by appointment.

Opening Hours: Mon–Sat, 10am–5pm. Sun, 1.30pm–4.30pm

Admission: Free

Facilities: Toilets, disabled access

ROYAL ARMOURIES

HOME OF THE NATIONAL COLLECTION OF ARMS AND ARMOUR

The Royal Armouries began life as the main royal and national arsenal housed in the Tower of London. Indeed the Royal Armouries has occupied buildings within the Tower for making and storing arms, armour and military equipment for as long as the Tower itself has been in existence.

Developed to supply the armies and navies of England 900 years ago, it is now one of the finest and largest collections of arms and armour in the world. The Royal Armouries can also claim with good justification to be Britain's oldest museum, since it developed as a public showplace for arms and armour from at least the time of the restoration of King Charles II in 1660.

It now has displays in its historic home at the White Tower in London, a purpose-built museum in Leeds, an artillery museum at Fort Nelson, near Portsmouth, and even a presence in the USA, at the Frazier Museum of International History, Louisville, Kentucky.

The Museum's collections span 3,000 years of history – and are still relevant to the issues of power and conflict we live with today.

Royal Armouries Museum, Armouries Drive, Leeds LS10 1LT
Opening hours: Daily 10am–5pm (Closed 24–26 December)
Admission: Entry to the Museum is free but some activities and events may be charged
Facilities: Toilets, café, disabled access, library and research facilities.

Fort Nelson, Portsdown Hill Road, Fareham, Hampshire PO17 6AN
Apr–Oct: Daily, 10am–5pm (except Wed 11am–5pm)
Nov–Mar: Daily, 10.30am–4pm (except Wed 11.30am–4pm) (Closed 24–26 Dec)
Admission: Entry to the Museum is free but some activities and events may be charged
Facilities: Toilets, café, ramps provide access to most parts of the Fort

White Tower, H M Tower of London, EC3N 4AB
Admission included in Tower of London entry fee.
March–Oct: Tues–Sat, 9am–5pm. Sun–Mon, 10am–5.30pm
Nov–Feb: Tues–Sat, 9am–4.30pm. Sun–Mon, 10am–4.30pm (Closed 24–26 Dec)

Master of the Armouries: Jonathon Riley
Museum Directors: Peter Armstrong, Steve Burt, Graeme Rimer

For more information about the museum and forthcoming events please visit our website
www.royalarmouries.org

Richmond

GREEN HOWARDS REGIMENTAL MUSEUM

Town centre location

Green Howards Regimental Museum,
Trinity Church Square, Richmond,
North Yorkshire DL10 4QN
T / F: 01748 826561
E: greenhowardsmus@aol.com
www.greenhowards.org.uk

Curator: Lynda Powell

Green Howards (Alexandra, Princess of Wales's Own Yorkshire Regiment), Alexandra Princess of Wales's Own Regiment of Yorkshire, Princess of Wales's Own (Yorkshire Regiment), 19th (1st Yorkshire North Riding) Regiment of Foot, 19th Regiment of Foot, Beauclerk's Regiment, Howard's Regiment, Sutton's Regiment, Erle's Regiment, Colonel Luttrell's Companies of Foot, North Riding Rifle Volunteer Corps, Princess of Wales's Own Yorkshire Regiment Territorial Battalions, Princess of Wales's Own Yorkshire Regiment Volunteer Battalions, North Yorkshire Regiment of Militia, North Yorkshire Light Infantry Regiment of Militia, North Yorkshire Rifles (Militia), Princess of Wales's Own (Yorkshire Regiment) Militia

An excellent collection of well-presented items on three floors illustrating the 300 year history of this famous Regiment and its close links with the North Riding of Yorkshire. Rich displays of uniforms, badges, headdress and silver are complemented by an extensive medal collection with an interactive computer guide. There are special cases dedicated to the Ladies of the Regiment, military sport and a new temporary exhibition is displayed each year. Access to the Regimental archive is available by appointment.

Opening Hours: Mon–Sat: 1am–4.30pm. Closed Sundays and 1 Dec–31 Jan.

Admission: Adults £3.50, Seniors £3, Children free if accompanied by an adult

Facilities: Shop, disabled access, resource centre. Adjacent parking

Rotherham

YORK AND LANCASTER REGIMENT MUSEUM

Short walk from both bus and railway stations. By car access from M1(north) at J35 and then A629 to Rotherham, from M1 (south) at J33 then A63, from A1 take A630

York and Lancaster Regiment Museum,
Central Library and Arts Centre,
Walker Place, Rotherham, South
Yorkshire S65 1JH
T: 01709 336633 / F: 01709 336628
E: yorkandlancsmuseum@rotherham.gov.uk
www.rotherham.gov.uk

Curator: Karl Noble

York and Lancaster Regiment, 65th (2nd Yorkshire North Riding) Regiment of Foot, 65th Regiment of Foot, 84th (York and Lancaster) Regiment of Foot, 84th Regiment of Foot, 84th Royal Highland Emigrant Corps, Eyre Coote's 84th Regiment of Foot

A comprehensive collection of uniforms, weapons, equipment and campaign relics traces the history of the Yorks and Lancs and its forebears the 65th and 84th Regiments of Foot from 1758 to 1968 through a chronological series of displays. Specific cases are dedicated to the Militia, Volunteers and Territorials, the Band, Silver and Sport. There is also a medals display which includes nine Victoria Crosses.

Opening Hours: Mon–Sat 9.30am–5pm. Closed Sun and Bank Holidays. NB: appointments must be made to speak to the Curator.

Admission: Free

Facilities: Toilets, refreshments, shop, disabled access. Adjacent parking

YORKSHIRE

York

KOHIMA MUSEUM

South of city centre, on A19 Fulford Road

Kohima Museum, Imphal Barracks,
Fulford Road, York YO10 4HD
T: 01904 665806 / 635212
E: thekohimamuseum@hotmail.com
www.kohimamuseum.com

Curator: Bob Cook

Kohima Garrison (1944), 2nd Infantry Division and 33 Indian Brigade (1944)

The collection commemorates the Battle of Kohima and follows the fortunes of the 2nd Division up to and including its role in crossing the Irrawady. Almost all the objects have been donated by veterans and their relatives making it a very personal collection that sees the battle through the eyes of those who fought it.

Opening Hours: Thu only 9am–12pm or by previous appointment

Admission: Free

Facilities: Parking, toilets, shop, disabled access

PRINCE OF WALES'S OWN REGIMENT OF YORKSHIRE MUSEUM

Centre of York, opposite Clifford's Tower. Approximately a 15-minute walk from the station

Prince of Wales's Own Regiment of Yorkshire Museum,
3 Tower Street, York YO1 9SB
T: 01904 461010 / F: 01904 658824
E: yorksregtaffairs@btconnect.com
www.pwo-yorkshire.museum

Curator: Major ML Sulliavan

Prince of Wales's Own Regiment of Yorkshire, West Yorkshire Regiment (The Prince of Wales's Own), Prince of Wales's Own (West Yorkshire Regiment), 14th (Buckinghamshire) (Prince of Wales's Own) Regiment of Foot, 14th (or the Buckinghamshire) Regiment of Foot, 14th (or the Bedfordshire) Regiment of Foot, 14th Regiment of Foot, Sir Edward Hales's Regiment of Foot, East Yorkshire Regiment (Duke of York's Own), East Yorkshire Regiment, 15th (or the Yorkshire East Riding) Regiment of Foot, 15th Regiment of Foot, Sir William Clifton's Regiment of Foot

The collection covers the history of two famous Yorkshire regiments, both raised in 1685 by King James II. Displays of uniforms, badges, medals, silver, weapons, trophies, pictures and photographs illustrate the lives and service of both regiments over a period of 300 years. Objects related to the successor regiment, The Prince of Wales's Own Regiment of Yorkshire, continue the story from 1958 and the most recent, 2006, amalgamation into The Yorkshire Regiment is also covered. The archives of the West Yorkshire Regiment and East Yorkshire Regiment are held by the Museum. They are not open to the public but enquiries and research can be undertaken by museum staff. The website address for the recently formed Yorkshire Regiment is www.yorkshireregiment.mod.uk.

The Museum is located in the same building as that of the Royal Dragoon Guards and the information given below applies to both collections.

Opening Hours: Mon–Fri, 9.30am–4.30pm. Saturday 10am–4pm. Closed from Christmas until the end of January

Admission: Adults £2, Seniors/Children £1. Groups and school parties by appointment

Facilities: Toilets, shop, disabled access. Adjacent parking

YORKSHIRE

For a detailed map, go to **www.streetmap.co.uk** and type in the postcode of the museum

QUEEN'S OWN YORKSHIRE YEOMANRY

South of city centre, on A19 Fulford Road

The Queen's Own Yorkshire Yeomanry Museum, Yeomanry Barracks, Fulford Road, York YO10 4ES
T: 01482 881974 / F: 01482 881974
E: pominic.peacock@nps.co.uk

Curator: Dominic Peacock

The Queen's Own Yorkshire Yeomanry, The Yorkshire Hussars, The Queen's Own Yorkshire Dragoons, the East Riding Yeomanry

A small collection of artefacts and memorabilia from Yorkshire's Yeomanry Regiments. The Museum can be visited by prior appointment with the Yorkshire Squadron Office of the Queen's Own Yeomanry which can be contacted on 01904 620320. For information on the collections and regimental records and to contact the Old Comrades Association please contact the Regimental Secretary, Dominic Peacock, on the telephone number and email address shown above.

ROYAL DRAGOON GUARDS

Centre of York, opposite Clifford's Tower. Approximately a 15-minute walk from the station

Royal Dragoon Guards Museum, 3 Tower Street, York YO1 9SB
T: 01904 642036 / F: 01904 642036
E: hhq@rdgmuseum.org.uk
www.rdgmuseum.org.uk

Curator: Captain WA Hensall

Royal Dragoon Guards), 4th Royal Irish Dragoon Guards, 4th (Royal Irish) Dragoon Guards, 7th Dragoon Guards (Princess Royal's), 7th (Princess Royal's) Dragoon Guards, 5th Royal Inniskilling Dragoons Guards,5th Inniskilling Dragoon Guards, 5th/6th Dragoons, 5th Dragoon Guards (Princess Charlotte of Wales's), 5th (Princess Charlotte of Wales's) Dragoon Guards,5th Dragoon Guards, Inniskilling (6th Dragoons), 6th (Inniskilling) Dragoons, 6th (Enniskilling) Regiment of Dragoons, 6th or Inniskilling Regiment of Dragoons, 6th (Inniskilling) Regiment of Dragoons.

The museum tells the story of the 4th/7th Royal Dragoon Guards from 1685, when six Troops of Horse were raised for service under King James II, and continues up to the Regiment's amalgamation with the 5th Royal Inniskilling Dragoon Guards to form the present Royal Dragoons Guards. It includes artefacts from all the antecedent regiments dating back to their formation in the 1680s. The regimental archive is held in the same building and may be viewed by appointment.

The museum is located in the same building as that of the Prince of Wales's Own Regiment of Yorkshire.

Opening Hours: Mon–Fri, 9.30am–4.30pm. Saturday 10am–4pm. Closed from Christmas until the end of January

Admission: Adults £2, Seniors/Children £1. Groups and school parties by appointment

Facilities: Toilets, shop, disabled access. Public Car Park 100m (opposite Hilton Hotel)

YORKSHIRE

North East

Alnwick

THE FUSILIERS MUSEUM OF NORTHUMBERLAND

Along old A1, or bus to town Market Place, then a short walk

The Fusiliers Museum of Northumberland
The Abbott's Tower, Alnwick Castle,
Alnwick, Northumberland NE66 1NG
T: 01665 602152 / F: 01665 605257
E:fusnorthld@aol.com
www.northumberlandfusiliers.org.uk

Curator: Captain Tony Adamson

Royal Regiment of Fusiliers, Royal Northumberland Fusiliers, Northumberland Fusiliers, 5th Regiment of Foot (Northumberland Fusiliers), 5th (or the Northumberland) Regiment of Foot, 5th Regiment of Foot, Lord O'Brien's Regiment (or the Irish Regiment)

The museum covers the history of the Royal Northumberland Fusiliers from its raising in 1674 up to and including its more recent post-1968 history as part of the Royal Regiment of Fusiliers. Housed on three floors of a tower in historic Alnwick Castle, the collection tells the story of this famous Regiment by reference to the lives of its soldiers, their families and the communities from which they came. The regimental archive and library may be viewed by appointment.

Opening Hours: Easter–Oct: daily 11am–5pm

Admission: Free after payment for entry to the Castle

Facilities: Shop, archives (by appointment)

Berwick-upon-Tweed

KING'S OWN SCOTTISH BORDERERS MUSEUM

On the Parade, near the town centre off Church Street

King's Own Scottish Borderers Regimental Museum, The Barracks, Berwick-upon-Tweed, Northumberland, TD15 1DG
T: 01289 307426 / F: 01289 331928
E: rhq.kosb@scotsborderers.army.co.uk
www.kosb.co.uk/museum.htm

Curator: Lt Col George Wood

King's Own Scottish Borderers, King's Own Borderers, 25th (or King's Own Borderers) Regiment of Foot, 25th (or the Sussex) Regiment of Foot, 25th (Edinburgh) Regiment of Foot, Earl of Leven's Regiment of Foot (The Edinburgh Regiment)

The museum covers the history of the Regiment from 1689 to the present day with displays of uniforms, badges, medals, weapons and relics from the various campaigns in which it has been involved. Tableaux and dioramas dramatically bring to life the Regiment's battles and aspects of the soldier's profession. The Regiment has an unrivalled collection of documents and pictures relating to over three centuries of Regimental history. Access to the archives may be arranged by prior appointment. Please contact the Museum for details.

Opening Hours: Open: Wed–Sun, 10am–5pm (1 April–30 Sept) Closed: 1 Oct–31 Mar

Admission: Adults £3.70, Concessions £3.10, Children (5–15 years) £1.90 under 5s free. Free admission for members of English Heritage and serving members of the Armed Forces. Reduced price for members of Historic Scotland and CADW.

Berwick Barracks is an English Heritage site. The admission charge provides access to the Regimental Museum, the exhibition 'By Beat of Drum', Berwick Town Museum and Art Gallery, and the Gymnasium Gallery of contemporary art.

Facilities: Toilets, shop, refreshments. Public car park nearby

NORTH EAST

Durham

DURHAM LIGHT INFANTRY MUSEUM

About half a mile from the railway station north of Durham City centre signposted off A691

The DLI Museum and Durham Art Gallery,
Aykley Heads, Durham City DH1 5TU
T: 0191 3842214 / F: 0191 3861770
E: dli@durham.gov.uk
www.durham.gov.uk/dli

Curator: Emma Hamlett

Durham Light Infantry, (Durham) Light Infantry, 68th (or the Durham) Regiment of Foot, 68th Regiment of Foot, 106th Bombay Light Infantry, 2nd European Regiment Bombay Light Infantry (Honourable East India Company), 2nd Bombay European Regiment of Foot (Honourable East India Company), Durham Militia, Rifle Volunteers and Home Guard

The museum tells the story of the Regiment from its raising in 1758 to its absorption into the Light Infantry in 1968, with particular emphasis on the two world wars. The displays focus on the experience of war using letter and diary extracts, plus the recorded voices of DLI soldiers, to describe the life of the Regiment in the context of the Durham community from which it was drawn. The regimental archive is in the Durham County Record Office (T: 0191 3833253), a short walk from the museum. The catalogue, including all photographs, is available online on the Record Office website.

'There may be some Regiments as good but I know of none better', Field Marshal Montgomery of Alamein.

Opening Hours: 1 Apr–31 Oct: 10am–5pm
1 Nov–31 Mar: 10am–4pm. Closed Christmas Eve and Day

Admission: Adults £3.50 (annual £4.50), Concessions £2.50 (annual £3.50), Children (5–16 years) £1.50 (annual £2.50). Special rates for groups and school parties.

Facilities: Parking, toilets, refreshments, shop, disabled access, lecture room, corporate events, picnic area

Gateshead

101 (NORTHUMBRIAN) REGIMENT ROYAL ARTILLERY (VOLUNTEERS) MUSEUM

1.5 miles south of the River Tyne, to the west of the A167

101 (Northumbrian) Regt RA(V) Museum,
Napier Armoury, Alexandra Road,
Tyne and Wear NE8 4HX
T: 0191 239 5237

Curator: Major C Whitley

A small collection covering the history of the Regiment.

Opening Hours: By appointment only

Admission: Free

Facilities: Parking, toilets, lecture room

Newcastle upon Tyne

THE LIGHT DRAGOONS (15TH/19TH KING'S ROYAL HUSSARS)

and

NORTHUMBERLAND HUSSARS MUSEUM COLLECTIONS

A short walk from Newcastle Central Station

A SOLDIER'S LIFE

Discovery Museum, Blandford Square,
Newcastle upon Tyne NE1 4JA
T: 0191 232 6789 / F: 0191 230 2614
E: roberta.goldwater@twmuseums.org.uk or
mail@lightdragoons.org.uk
www.twmuseums.org.uk

Curator: Captain CN Bird

The Light Dragoons, 15th/19th King's Royal Hussars, 15th King's Hussars, 15th (King's) Light Dragoons, 1st (King's Royal) Light Dragoons, 15th Light Dragoons (Eliott's Light Horse), 19th Royal Hussars (Queen Alexandra's Own), 19th (Prince of Wales's Own) Hussars, 19th Hussars Bengal European Light Cavalry (Honourable East India Company), 19th Light Dragoons (Drogheda's Horse), Northumberland Hussars, Northumberland & Newcastle Volunteer Cavalry Imperial Yeomanry (1900-1902), 108th (NH) Anti-Tank Regiment RA, 274th (NH) Light Anti-Aircraft Battery RA Queen's Own Yeomanry

The regimental collections are on display in the Soldier's Life Gallery of the Discovery Museum and that theme characterises the displays which reflect the various stages of a soldier's life in a cavalry regiment. These include recruitment, training, life in war and peace, death and retirement. The objects on display include uniforms, badges and regimental memorabilia. There is extensive use of realistic mannequins and evocative scene setting as well as a short film of life in The Light Dragoons. The Gallery has recently undergone major refurbishment and houses an excellent, well presented collection.

Opening Hours: Mon–Sat 10am–5pm, Sun 2–5pm

Admission: Free

Facilities: Parking, toilets, refreshments, shop, disabled access, corporate events

NORTH EAST

Northern Ireland

118 ■Belfast

119

116 117

Armagh:	116	Royal Irish Fusiliers
	117	Royal Irish Regiment
Belfast:	118	Royal Ulster Rifles
Enniskillen:	119	Royal Inniskilling Fusiliers

Armagh

ROYAL IRISH FUSILIERS MUSEUM 116

Sovereign's House can be found at one end of The Mall about 20 metres from the Court House and a 5-minute walk from the Translink Bus station

Royal Irish Fusiliers Regimental Museum, Sovereign's House, The Mall, Armagh, Co. Armagh BT61 9DL
T: 0283 752 2911 / F: 0283 752 2911
E: fusiliersmuseum@yahoo.co.uk

Curator: Amanda Moreno

Royal Irish Regiment, Royal Irish Rangers, Royal Irish Fusiliers (Princess Victoria's), Princess Victoria's (Royal Irish Fusiliers), 87th (or Royal Irish Fusiliers) Regiment of Foot, 87th (Prince of Wales's Own Irish Fusiliers) Regiment of Foot, 87th (or Prince of Wales's Own Irish) Regiment of Foot, 89th (Princess Victoria's) Regiment of Foot, 89th Regiment of Foot, Armagh, Cavan and Monaghan Militias

The museum is housed in the grade B+ Sovereign's House. The Eagle Takers Gallery won the Best Exhibition in Ireland in 2003. The collection contains the uniforms, medals, regalia and the two Victoria Crosses won by the Regiment. The Regimental archive and library may be viewed by appointment.

Opening Hours: Mon–Fri (inc. Bank Holidays) 10am–12.30pm and 1.30–4pm. Closed Christmas Day and New Years Day

Admission: Free

Facilities: Toilets, shop, lecture room

ROYAL IRISH REGIMENT MUSEUM 117

Royal Irish Regiment Museum – Closed
For enquiries please contact:
Royal Irish Fusiliers Museum, Sovereign's House, The Mall, Armagh, BT61 9DL
T. 028 37522911
E. fusiliersmuseum@yahoo.co.uk
www.army.mod.uk/infantry/regiments/royalirish

Curator: Captain Mark Hagan

The Royal Irish Regiment (27th (INNISKILLING) 83rd, 87th and The Ulster Defence Regiment), Royal Irish Rangers (27th, 83rd, 86th, 87th, 89th and 108th Foot), Ulster Defence Regiment

The Museum is currently closed, pending relocation. The collection traces the history of the Regiment from the raising of its most senior antecedent, the Royal Inniskilling Fusiliers in 1689, to the present day, with an emphasis on the activities of the Royal Irish Regiment and its immediate predecessors the Royal Irish Rangers and the Ulster Defence Regiment.

For enquiries during the closure please contact the Royal Irish Fusiliers Museum.

Belfast

ROYAL ULSTER RIFLES MUSEUM 118

Close to the city centre in the cathedral quarter

Royal Ulster Rifles Museum, 5 Waring Street
Belfast BT1 2EW
T: 028 9023 2086 / F: 028 9023 2086
E: rurmuseum@yahoo.co.uk
www.435728.com

Museum Attendant: RGT Nelson

Royal Irish Regiment, Royal Irish Rangers, Royal Ulster Rifles, Royal Irish Rifles, 83rd (County of Dublin) Regiment of Foot, 83rd Regiment of Foot (Fitch's Grenadiers), 86th (Royal County Down) Regiment of Foot, 86th Regiment of Foot (Cuyler's Shropshire Volunteers)

The Museum houses an extensive collection of uniforms, badges, medals and regimental memorabilia covering the history of the Regiment and the campaigns in which it has fought since its formation in 1793. The collection is well supported by digitised records and books.

Opening Hours: Targets: Mon–Fri, 10am–12.30pm and 2pm–4pm (2.30pm on Fri). Visitors are strongly advised to confirm opening times by telephone in advance.

Admission: Adults £1. Free to serving and former members of the Regiment, Seniors and Children

Facilities: Shop, limited disabled access

Enniskillen

ROYAL INNISKILLING FUSILIERS MUSEUM

South of town centre overlooking the River Erne. Well signposted

Royal Inniskilling Fusiliers Museum
The Castle, Enniskillen,
Co Fermanagh BT74 7HL
T: 028 6632 3142 / F: 028 6632 0359
E: info@inniskillingsmuseum.com
www.inniskillingsmuseum.com

Curator: Major JM Dunlop

Royal Irish Regiment, Royal Irish Rangers, Royal Inniskilling Fusiliers, 27th (Inniskilling) Regiment of Foot, Colonel Zachariah Tiffin's Enniskillen Regiment of Foot, 108th (Madras Infantry) Regiment of Foot, 3rd (Madras) European Regiment (Honourable East India Company), The Fermanagh, Donegal and Tyrone Militias

Enniskillen is the only town in the United Kingdom to have given its name to two regiments, and this museum is an important Regimental collection telling their story. The Royal Inniskilling Fusiliers (Colonel Zachariah Tiffin's Regiment, then 27th (Inniskilling) Regiment of Foot) originated in 1688–9, and their story is told down to amalgamation in 1968 and beyond, to their successor The Royal Irish Regiment. Founded at the same time, the 5th Royal Inniskilling Dragoon Guards (Colonel Albert Conyingham's Horse, then 6th Inniskilling Dragoons) have their own story told down to amalgamation in 1992. The very recently modernised Museum features a wide range of original uniforms, weapons, silver, medals and Regimental memorabilia including eight Victoria Crosses awarded during World War I and the bugle that sounded the advance of the 36th (Ulster) Division at the opening of the Battle of the Somme on 1 July 1916. The collection is displayed in chronological order in the Keep of Enniskillen Castle. The footprint of this keep goes back to the Tower House of the 15th Century Gaelic clan, the Maguires. A further part of the collection including military vehicles, a Great War First Aid Station and a Dragoons Blacksmiths Shop are housed in the former stables of the 18th-century Cavalry Barracks adjacent to the Keep. The courtyard features Napoleonic cannons and German artillery guns. On the ground floor, easily accessible by wheel chair, is a virtual tour on a screen monitor, which tells the story of the Regiments, and shows images of the Museum on the upper two floors. An extensive regimental library and archive may be viewed by appointment with the Curator.

Opening Times: May, Jun and Sep: Mon and Sat 2pm–5pm, Tue–Fri 10am–5pm. Jul and Aug: Mon, Sat and Sun 2pm–5pm. Oct–Apr: Mon 2pm–5pm, Tue–Fri 10am–5pm. Open Bank Holidays 10am–5pm

Admission: Adults £3.50, Children and Senior Citizens £2.50, School parties £2pp. Groups (10+) £3pp. Family ticket £9.50.

Facilities: Parking, toilets, shop, AV virtual tour for visitors with a disability

Scotland

Inverness `125`

120

`128`

`122`

`129`

Edinburgh

Glasgow `123` `124`

`126` `127`

`121`

SCOTLAND

Aberdeen

THE GORDON HIGHLANDERS MUSEUM

2.5 miles west of the city. No 14, X15 and X17 bus from Union Street to Queen's Road/Viewfield Road

 The Gordon Highlanders Museum, St Luke's, Viewfield Road, Aberdeen AB15 7XH
T: 01224 311200 / F: 01224 319323
E: museum@gordonhighlanders.com
www.gordonhighlanders.com

Executive Director: Claire Petty
Curator: Jesper Ericsson

The Highlanders (Seaforth, Gordons and Camerons), Gordon Highlanders, 75th (Stirlingshire) Regiment of Foot, 75th Regiment of Foot, 75th (Highland) Regiment of Foot (Abercromby's Highlanders), 92nd (Gordon Highlanders) Regiment of Foot, 92nd (Highland) Regiment of Foot, 100th (Gordon Highlanders) Regiment of Foot, The London Scottish (Gordon Highlanders)

The Museum, which is a Visit Scotland five-star credited museum, houses an important collection of uniforms, badges, medals and regimental memorabilia illustrating the history of this famous Highland Regiment from the Napoleonic Wars through to recent operations in support of the United Nations. The exhibitions include interactive displays, sound stations, films, and models illustrating the deeds for which this Regiment is renowned. The full regimental archive is kept on site and access is available by appointment with the curator. There is also a programme of educational and recreation events and activities for all ages.

Opening Hours: Mon Closed. First Tues Apr to last Sun Sep: Tues–Sat, 10am–4.30pm, Sun 12.30pm–4.30pm. Oct, Nov, Feb and Mar: Tues–Sat 10am–4.00pm. Dec and Jan open by appointment only.

Admission: Adults £5, Seniors £3, Children £2. Family ticket £11 (2+2).

Facilities: Parking, toilets, tea-room, shop, garden, disabled access, corporate events and meetings

Ayr

AYRSHIRE YEOMANRY MUSEUM

 Ayrshire Yeomanry Museum, Rozelle House Galleries, Monument Road, Ayr KA7 4NQ
T: 01292 445447 / F: 01292 442065
E: ayryeomuseum@googlemail.com

Curator: Major Christopher Roads

Ayrshire (Earl of Carrick's Own) Yeomanry

The Museum collection traces the history of the Regiment from its formation in 1793, through its service as cavalry in South Africa, infantry in World War I and artillery in World War II. The displays include uniformed figures, medals, weapons, maps, photographs, paintings and memorabilia from the Regiment's various campaigns. The Regiment is now part of the Queen's Own Yeomanry.

Opening Hours: Mon–Sun, 10am–5pm. Closed Sundays, Nov–Mar.

Admission: Free

Facilities: Parking, toilets, refreshments, shop, corporate events

Cupar

FIFE AND FORFAR YEOMANRY COLLECTION

 Fife and Forfar Yeomanry Collection, Yeomanry House, Castlebank Road, Cupar, Fife HY15 4BL
T: 01334 656155
E: qoy-csqn-psa@mod.uk

Curator: Captain J Preece

A small Regimental collection, library and archive to which admission is by appointment only.

Facilities: Parking, toilets, lecture room

SCOTLAND

Edinburgh

THE ROYAL SCOTS DRAGOON GUARDS MUSEUM

Located within Edinburgh Castle

The Royal Scots Dragoon Guards Museum,
The Castle, Edinburgh EH1 2YT
T: 0131 310 5100 / F: 0131 310 5101
E: homehq@scotsdg.org.uk
www.scotsdgmuseum.com

Regimental Secretary:
Lieutenant Colonel RJ Binks

The Royal Scots Dragoon Guards (Carabiniers and Greys) 1971 from Royal Scots Greys (2nd Dragoons) and 3rd Carabiniers (Prince of Wales's Dragoon Guards).

Antecedent Regiments:3rd Carabiniers, 1928 from 3rd/6th Dragoon Guards, 1922 3rd Dragoon Guards (Prince of Wales's), previously 3rd (Prince of Wales's) Dragoon Guards, 3rd Regiment of Dragoon Guards and 4th Regiment of Horse, 1922 The Carabiniers (6th Dragoon Guards), previously 6th Dragoon Guards (The Carabiniers), 3rd Irish Horse, 7th Horse, King's Carabiniers, 8th Horse, 9th Regiment of Horse, Royal Scots Greys previously named Royal North British Dragoons, Royal Regiment of Scots Dragoons

An important collection illustrating the history of Scotland's only cavalry regiment and its English and Scottish antecedents dating back to 1678. Famous episodes in regimental history, such as the charge of the Royal Scots Greys at the Battle of Waterloo in 1815, the same Regiment's action in the 1943 Italian campaign and the 3rd Carabiniers epic assault in Burma are given pride of place amongst well presented displays of uniformed figures, paintings, photographs and regimental trophies from its various campaigns. Interactive displays and exhibits take the visitor right up to the Regiment's most recent involvement in Iraq. The regimental archive and library may be viewed by appointment with the Regimental Secretary.

Opening Hours: Daily 9.30am–5.30pm (4.30pm in Winter: Oct–Mar)

Admission: Free after payment of Castle entry charge. Groups and school parties by appointment only

Facilities: Toilets, refreshments and Shop (0131 220 4387) within Edinburgh Castle. Limited parking

ROYAL SCOTS REGIMENTAL MUSEUM

Located within Edinburgh Castle

Royal Scots Regimental Museum,
The Castle, Edinburgh EH1 2YT
T: 0131 310 5016 / F: 0131 310 5019
E: rhqrs@btconnect.com
www.theroyalscots.co.uk

Curator: Lieutenant Colonel WJ Blythe

Royal Scots (The Royal Regiment), Royal Scots (The Lothian Regiment), Lothian Regiment (Royal Scots), 1st or The Royal Scots Regiment, Royal Regiment of Foot, 1st Regiment of Foot or Royal Scots, 1st or Royal Regiment of Foot, Royal Regiment of Foot, Earl of Dumbarton's Regiment (1st Foot), Le Regiment de Douglas, Le Regiment d'Hebron

This Regiment, raised for King Charles 1st by Sir John Hepburn in 1633, is the oldest in the British Army. The museum illustrates its history chronologically through displays of paintings, artefacts, uniforms, silver, badges and medals. The Regimental archive and library are on site and may be viewed by appointment.

Opening Hours: Mon–Fri 9.30am–5pm in summer, 9.30am–3.45pm in winter. Closed Christmas and New Year

Admission: Free after payment of Castle entry charge

Facilities: Parking, toilets, refreshments, shop, lecture room

For a detailed map, go to www.streetmap.co.uk and type in the postcode of the museum

Fort George

THE HIGHLANDERS' MUSEUM

15 miles east of Inverness

The Highlanders' Museum,
Fort George, Ardersier,
Inverness-shire IV2 2TD
T: 0131 310 8701
E: thehighlandersmuseum@btconnect.com
www.thehighlandersmuseum.com

Curator: Dr Alix Powers-Jones

The Highlanders (Seaforth, Gordons, Camerons),Queen's Own Highlanders (Ross-shire Buffs, The Duke of Albany's), 72nd (or The Duke of Albany's Own Highlanders) Regiment of Foot, 72nd Regiment of Foot, 72nd (Highland) Regiment of Foot, 78th (Highland) Regiment of Foot (or the Ross-shire Buffs), 78th Regiment of (Highland) Foot, Queen's Own Cameron Highlanders, 79th Queen's Own Cameron Highlanders, 79th Regiment of Foot (or Cameron Highlanders), 79th Regiment of Foot (or Cameronian Highlanders), 79th Regiment of Foot (or Cameronian Volunteers), Lovat Scouts, Liverpool Scottish, 51st Highland Volunteers

The Regimental Museum Collection of the Queen's Own Highlanders is the private collection of a regiment with over 200 years association with Fort George. The Museum comprises a unique collection of medals, uniforms and accoutrements, weapons, paintings and prints, colours and pipe banners, mess plate, ceramics, and other artefacts covering the history of the Regiment back to 1778. The Museum also has a comprehensive library and archive collection to which researchers are welcome, and this includes original sources and published material on Fort George.

Opening Hours: Apr–Sep: daily 9.30am–5.15pm. Oct–Mar: Mon–Fri 10am–4pm. Closed Christmas and New Year

Admission: Free after payment of Fort George entry charge

Facilities: Parking, toilets, refreshments, shop, disabled access, lecture room

Glasgow

ROYAL HIGHLAND FUSILIERS MUSEUM

75 yards east of Charing Cross, bus to Charing Cross from Central Station

Royal Highland Fusiliers Museum,
518 Sauchiehall Street, Glasgow G2 3LW
T: 0141 332 5639 / F: 0141 353 1493
E: assregsec@rhf.org.uk
www.rhf.org.uk

Curator: Colonel RL Steele

Royal Highland Fusiliers(Princess Margaret's Own Glasgow & Ayrshire Regiment), Royal Scots Fusiliers, 21st (Royal Scots Fusiliers) Regiment of Foot, 21st Regiment of Foot (or Royal North British Fuzileers), Royal Regiment of North British Fuzileers, North British Fuzileers, The Earl of Mar's Regiment of Foot, Highland Light Infantry (City of Glasgow Regiment), 71st (Highland Light Infantry), 71st (Highland) Regiment of Foot (Light Infantry), 71st (Glasgow Highland) Regiment of Foot (Light Infantry), 71st (Glasgow Highland) Regiment of Foot, 71st (Highland) Regiment of Foot, 73rd (Highland) Regiment of Foot – MacLeod's Highlanders, 74th (Highland) Regiment of Foot, 74th Regiment of Foot, 74th (Highland) Regiment of Foot –The Assaye Regiment, Glasgow Highlanders (9th Bn Highland Light Infantry)

The Museum traces the history of the three regiments from which the Royal Highland Fusiliers are descended. Starting in 1678 the story carries through to the Regiment today. The collection is shown chronologically on two floors of interlinked galleries illustrating the many campaigns in which the Regiment has served with displays of weapons, uniforms, medals, music and regimental trophies and memorabilia. There is a good mix of artefacts, pictures, text and video screens. The regimental archive and library are held in the same building and may be viewed by appointment.

The building is of interest to those aware of Scottish design. The external façade and many of the interior details remain intact and reflect the style and influence of Charles Rennie Mackintosh.

Opening Hours: Mon–Fri, 8.30am–4pm. Weekends and evenings by appointment

Admission: Free. Groups and school parties by appointment

Facilities: Toilets, shop, disabled access, lecture room

Hamilton

CAMERONIANS (SCOTTISH RIFLES) MUSEUM COLLECTION

Exit M74 at J6, right at first roundabout, across second, right at third to car park immediately on the left

 Cameronians (Scottish Rifles) Museum Collection, Low Parks Museum, 129 Muir Street, Hamilton, South Lanarkshire ML3 6BJ
T: 01698 328232 / F: 01698 328412
E: lowparksmuseum@ southlanarkshire.gov.uk
www.cameronians.org

Curator: Gareth Hunt

Cameronians (Scottish Rifles), 26th (or Cameronian) Regiment of Foot, 26th Regiment of Foot, Earl of Angus's Regiment of Foot, 90th Light Infantry Regiment Perthshire Volunteers, 90th Regiment of Foot (or Perthshire Volunteers), 90th Perthshire Light Infantry, Lanarkshire Volunteers, Militia and Yeomanry Units

The Cameronians, formed in 1881 from the merger of the 26th and 90th Regiments of Foot, have a unique facet to their history, being the only regiment of the British Army to have a religious origin. Raised from Covenanters in 1698, the collection includes objects from the Covenanting period and from every major campaign in which the Regiment served until it disbanded in 1968, in preference to amalgamation, during a period of Army restructuring. Access to the archives (uncatalogued) is available by appointment.

Opening Hours: Mon–Sat 10am–5pm, Sun 12pm–5pm

Admission: Free

Facilities: Parking, toilets, shop, disabled access, lecture room, corporate events, civil weddings

Perth

THE MUSEUM OF THE BLACK WATCH

Well signed and within easy walking distance of the city centre

 The Museum of the Black Watch
Balhousie Castle, Hay Street, Perth PH1 5HR
T: 01738 638 152 / F: 01738.643.245
E: museum@theblackwatch.co.uk
www.theblackwatch.co.uk

Collections Manager: Emma Halford-Forbes

The Black Watch (Royal Highland Regiment), 42nd Royal Highland Regiment of Foot (The Black Watch), 42nd (The Royal Highland) Regiment of Foot, 42nd Regiment of Foot, Earl of Crawford's Regiment of Foot (The Highland Regiment), 73rd (Perthshire) Regiment of Foot, 73rd Regiment of Foot, 73rd (Highland) Regiment of Foot

The Collection covers the long history of the oldest of the Highland Regiments from its raising as six independent companies in 1725, until 2006 when it became a battalion of the Royal Regiment of Scotland. Displayed chronologically in seven rooms, each dedicated to a particular period in the Regiment's history, there are colours, uniforms, weapons, badges, medals, paintings and regimental trophies and artefacts illustrating some of the Regiment's many campaigns including the North American wars, the Napoleonic campaign, the Crimea, both world wars and more recent operations.

Opening Hours: Apr–Oct: Mon–Sat 9.30am–5pm, Sun 10am–3.30pm. Nov to Mar: Mon–Sat 9.30am–5pm

Admission: Adult £4; Concessions £3; Children (5–16) £2, (under 5) free; Family ticket £5, Royal Regiment of Scotland free; HM Forces £3

Facilities: Parking, toilets, shop

For a detailed map, go to www.streetmap.co.uk and type in the postcode of the museum

Stirling

ARGYLL AND SUTHERLAND HIGHLANDERS REGIMENTAL MUSEUM

Located in Stirling Castle

Argyll and Sutherland Highlanders Regimental Museum,
The Castle, Stirling FK8 1EH
T: 01786 475165 / F: 01786 446038
E: museum@argylls.co.uk
www.argylls.co.uk

Curator: Joyce Steele
Assistant Curator: Rod McKenzie

Argyll and Sutherland Highlanders (Princess Louise's), Princess Louise's (Argyll and Sutherland Highlanders), 91st (Princess Louise's Argyllshire Highlanders) Regiment of Foot, 91st (Argyllshire Highlanders) Regiment of Foot, 91st (Argyllshire) Regiment of Foot, 91st Regiment of Foot, 91st (Argyllshire) Regiment of Foot (Highlanders), 98th (Argyllshire) Regiment of Foot (Highlanders), 93rd (Sutherland Highlanders) Regiment of Foot, 93rd (Highland) Regiment of Foot

This rich collection covers the history of the Regiment from its raising in Stirling in 1794. It occupies eight rooms and is divided into periodical sections which include the Crimea where the Regiment formed 'The Thin Red Line', the Indian Mutiny, the Boer War, both World Wars, Korea, Suez, Aden, Malaya and the Regiments more recent operational deployments. Stories of military courage and gallantry are set in the human context of the Scottish communities from which the Regiment drew its soldiers and its strength. Objects on display include personal items, Regimental Colours, pipe banners, silver, trophies, medals and various items of period uniform and equipment, paintings and prints with an emphasis on associated eye-witness accounts and related anecdotes. There are dioramas and a realistic model of a World War I trench. Access to the archives is available by appointment. Historical enquiries regarding the Regiment or museum can be sent to the postal or e-mail addresses above.

Opening Hours: Easter–Sep: Daily 9.30am–5pm. Oct–Easter: Daily 10am–4.15pm

Admission: Free, after payment for Castle entry

Facilities: Parking, refreshments, shop. Toilets available in the Castle

All information is correct at the time of going to press, but **you are advised to contact museums before making a visit**

SCOTLAND

93

Part II
Regimental Index

Succession of Titles

Household Cavalry

THE LIFE GUARDS

1881   1st Life Guards and 2nd Life Guards
1922   The Life Guards

THE BLUES AND ROYALS
(ROYAL HORSE GUARDS AND 1ST DRAGOONS)

1881   Royal Horse Guards (The Blues)
1968   The Blues and Royals (Royal Horse Guards and 1st
       Dragoons)

1881   1st (Royal) Dragoons
1921   1st The Royal Dragoons
1961   The Royal Dragoons (1st Dragoons)
1968   The Blues and Royal (Royal Horse Guards and 1st
       Dragoons)

Royal Armoured Corps

1ST THE QUEEN'S DRAGOON GUARDS

1881   1st King's Dragoon Guards
1959   1st The Queen's Dragoon Guards

1881   2nd Dragoon Guards (Queen's Bays)
1921   The Queen's Bays (2nd Dragoon Guards)
1959   1st The Queen's Dragoon Guards

THE ROYAL SCOTS DRAGOON GUARD
(CARABINIERS AND GREYS)

1881   3rd (Prince of Wales's) Dragoon Guards
1922   3rd/6th Dragoon Guards
1928   3rd Carabiniers (Prince of Wales's Dragoon Guards)
1971   The Royal Scots Dragoon Guards (Carabiniers and
       Greys)

1881   6th Dragoon Guards (Carabiniers)
1922   3rd/6th Dragoon Guards
1928   3rd Carabiniers (Prince of Wales's Dragoon Guards)
1971   The Royal Scots Dragoon Guards (Carabiniers and
       Greys)
1881   2nd Dragoon (Royal Scots Greys)
1921   The Royal Scots Greys (2nd Dragoons)
1971   The Royal Scots Dragoon Guards (Carabiniers and Greys)

THE ROYAL DRAGOON GUARDS

1881   4th Royal Irish Dragoon Guards
1922   4th/7th Dragoon Guards
1936   4th/7th Royal Dragoon Guards
1992   Royal Dragoon Guards

1881   7th (The Princess Royal's) Dragoon Guards
1921   7th Dragoon Guards (Princess Royal's)
1922   4th/th Dragoon Guards
1936   4th/7th Royal Dragoon Guards
1992   The Royal Dragoon Guards

1881   5th (Princess Charlotte of Wales's) Dragoon Guards
1921   5th Dragoon Guards (Princess Charlotte of Wales's)
1922   5th/6th Dragoons
1927   5th Inniskilling Dragoon Guards
1936   5th Royal Inniskilling Dragoon Guards
1992   The Royal Dragoon Guards

1881   6th (Inniskilling) Dragoons
1921   The Inniskillings (6th Dragoons)
1922   5th/6th Dragoons
1927   5th Inniskilling Dragoon Guards
1936   5th Royal Inniskilling Dragoon Guards
1992   The Royal Dragoon Guards

THE QUEEN'S ROYAL HUSSARS
(THE QUEEN'S OWN AND ROYAL IRISH)

1881   3rd (King's Own) Hussars
1921   3rd The King's Own Hussars
1958   The Queen's Own Hussars
1993   The Queen's Royal Hussars

1881   7th (Queen's Own) Hussars
1921   7th Queen's Own Hussars
1958   The Queen's Own Hussars
1993   Queen's Royal Hussars

1881   4th (Queen's Own) Hussars
1921   4th Queen's Own Hussars
1958   The Queen's Royal Irish Hussars
1993   The Queen's Royal Hussars

1881   8th (King's Royal Irish) Hussars
1921   8th King's Royal Irish Hussars
1958   The Queen's Royal Irish Hussars
1993   The Queen's Royal Hussars

9TH/12TH ROYAL LANCERS (PRINCE OF WALES'S)

1881 9th (Queen's Royal) Lancers
1921 9th Queen's Royal Lancers
1959 9th/12th Royal Lancers (Prince of Wales's)

1881 12th (Prince of Wales's Royal) Lancers
1921 12th Royal Lancers (Prince of Wales's)
1959 9th/12th Royal Lancers (Prince of Wales's)

THE KING'S ROYAL HUSSARS

1881 10th (Prince of Wales Own Royal) Hussars
1921 10th Royal Hussars (Prince of Wales's Own)
1969 The Royal Hussars (Prince of Wales Own)
1992 The King's Royal Hussars

1881 11th (or Prince Albert's Own) Hussars
1921 11th Hussars (Prince Albert's Own)
1969 The Royal Hussars (Prince of Wales's Own)
1992 The King's Royal Hussars

1881 14th (King's) Hussars
1921 14th King's Hussars
1922 14th/20th Hussars
1936 14th/20th King's Hussars
1992 The King's Royal Hussars

1881 20th Hussars
1923 14th/20th Hussars
1936 14th/20th King's Hussars
1992 The King's Royal Hussars

THE LIGHT DRAGOONS

1881 13th Hussars
1922 13th/18th Hussars
1935 13th/18th Royal Hussars (Queen Mary's Own)
1992 The Light Dragoons

1881 18th Hussars
1903 18th (Princess of Wales's Own) Hussars
1905 18th (Victoria Mary, Princess of Wales's Own) Hussars
1910 18th (Queen Mary's Own) Hussars
1919 18th (Queen Mary's Own) Royal Hussars
1921 18th Royal Hussars (Queen Mary's Own)
1922 13th/18th Hussars
1935 13th/18th Royal Hussars (Queen Mary's Own)
1992 The Light Dragoons

1881 15th (The King's) Hussars
1921 15th The King's Hussars
1922 15th/19th Hussars
1932 15th The King's Royal Hussars

1933 15th/19th The King's Royal Hussars
1992 The Light Dragoons

1881 19th Hussars
1902 19th (Queen Alexandra's Own Royal) Hussars
1921 19th Royal Hussars (Queen Alexandra's Own)
1922 15th/19th Hussars
1932 15th The King's Royal Hussars
1933 15th/19th The King's Royal Hussars
1992 The Light Dragoons

THE QUEEN'S ROYAL LANCERS

1881 16th (or Queen's) Lancers
1905 16th (The Queen's) Lancers
1921 16th The Queen's Lancers
1922 16th/5th Lancers
1954 16th/5th The Queen's Royal Lancers
1993 The Queen's Royal Lancers

1881 5th (Royal Irish) Lancers
1921 5th Royal Irish Lancers
1922 16th/5th Lancers
1954 16th/5th The Queen's Royal Lancers
1993 The Queen's Royal Lancers

1881 17th (Duke of Cambridge's Own) Lancers
1921 17th Lancers (Duke of Cambridge's Own)
1922 17th/21st Lancers
1993 The Queen's Royal Lancers

1881 21st Hussars
1897 21st Lancers
1898 21st Lancers (Empress of India's)
1922 17th/21st Lancers
1993 The Queen's Royal Lancers

ROYAL TANK REGIMENT

1917 The Tank Corps
1923 Royal Tank Corps
1939 Royal Tank Regiment

Foot Guards

GRENADIER GUARDS

COLDSTREAM GUARDS

SCOTS GUARDS

IRISH GUARDS (raised 1900)

WELSH GUARDS (raised 1915)

Infantry of the Line

ROYAL REGIMENT OF SCOTLAND

Royal Scots Borderers, 1st Btn

The Royal Scots
1881   The Lothian Regiment (Royal Scots)
1881   The Royal Scots (The Lothian Regiment)
1920   The Royal Scots (The Royal Regiment) (1st Foot)
2006   1st Battalion, Royal Regiment of Scotland

King's Own Scottish Borderers
1881   The King's Own Borderers
1881   The King's Own Scottish Borderers
2006   1st Battalion, Royal Regiment of Scotland

Royal Highland Fusiliers, 2nd Btn

21   **Royal Scots Fusiliers**
        1881   The Royal Scots Fusiliers
        1959   Royal Highland Fusiliers
        2006   2nd Battalion, Royal Regiment of Scotland

71 & 74 **Highland Light Infantry**
        1881   The Highland Light Infantry
        1923   The Highland Light Infantry (City of Glasgow Regiment)
        1959   Royal Highland Fusiliers
        2006   2nd Battalion, Royal Regiment of Scotland

The Black Watch, 3rd Btn

42 & 73 **The Black Watch**
        1881   The Black Watch (The Royal Highland Regiment)
        2006   3rd Battalion, Royal Regiment of Scotland

The Highlanders, 4th Btn

72 & 78 **Seaforth Highlanders**
        1881   Seaforth Highlanders (Ross-shire Buffs, Duke of Albany's Own)
        1961   Queen's Own Highlanders (Seaforth and Camerons)
        1994   The Highlanders (Seaforth, Gordons and Camerons)
        2006   4th Battalion, Royal Regiment of Scotland

Queen's Own Cameron Highlanders
1881   Queen's Own Cameron Highlanders
1961   Queen's own Highlanders (Seaforth and Camerons)

1994   The Highlanders (Seaforth, Gordons and Camerons)
2006   4th Battalion, Royal Regiment of Scotland

75 & 92 **Gordon Highlanders**
        1881   Gordon Highlanders
        1994   The Highlanders (Seaforth, Gordons and Camerons)
        2006   4th Battalion, Royal Regiment of Scotland

Argyll and Sutherland Highlanders, 5th Btn

91 & 93 **Argyll and Sutherland Highlanders**
        1881   Princess Louise's (Argyll and Sutherland Highlanders)
        1920   Argyll and Sutherland Highlanders (Princess Louise's)
        2006   5th Battalion, Argyll and Sutherland Highlanders

PRINCESS OF WALES'S ROYAL REGIMENT

2   1881   The Royal West Surrey Regiment (The Queen's)
        1881   The Queen's (Royal West Surrey Regiment)
        1921   The Queen's Royal Regiment (West Surrey)
        1959   The Queen's Royal Surrey Regiment
        1966   The Queen's Regiment
        1992   The Princess of Wales's Royal Regiment (Queen's and Royal Hampshires)

31 & 70 1881   The East Surrey Regiment
        1959   The Queen's Royal Surrey Regiment
        1966   The Queen's Regiment
        1992   The Princess of Wales's Royal Regiment (Queen's and Royal Hampshires)

3   1881   The Buffs (East Kent Regiment)
        1935   The Buffs (Royal East Kent Regiment)
        1960   The Queen's Own Buffs, The Royal Kent Regiment
        1966   The Queen's Regiment
        1992   The Princess of Wales's Royal Regiment (Queen's and Royal Hampshires)

50 & 97 1881   The Queen's Own (Royal West Kent Regiment)
        1921   The Royal West Kent Regiment (Queen's Own)
        1922   The Queen's Own Royal West Kent Regiment
        1961   The Queen's Own Buffs, Royal Kent Regiment
        1966   The Queen's Regiment
        1992   The Princess of Wales's Royal Regiment (Queen's and Royal Hampshires)

35 & 107 1881   The Royal Sussex Regiment
        1966   The Queen's Regiment
        1992   The Princess of Wales's Royal Regiment (Queen's and Royal Hampshires)

57 & 77	1881	The Duke of Cambridge's Own (Middlesex Regiment)
	1921	The Middlesex Regiment (Duke of Cambridge's Own)
	1966	The Queen's Regiment
	1992	The Princess of Wales's Royal Regiment (Queen's and Royal Hampshires)
37 & 67	1881	The Hampshire Regiment
	1946	The Royal Hampshire Regiment
	1992	The Princess of Wales's Royal Regiment (Queen's and Royal Hampshires)

THE DUKE OF LANCASTER'S REGIMENT

4	1881	The King's Own (Royal Lancaster Regiment)
	1921	The King's Own Royal Regiment (Lancaster)
	1959	The King's Own Royal Border Regiment
	2006	The Duke of Lancaster's Regiment
34 & 55	1881	The Border Regiment
	1959	The King's Own Royal Border Regiment
	2006	The Duke of Lancaster's Regiment
8	1881	The King's (Liverpool Regiment)
	1921	The King's Regiment (Liverpool)
	1958	The King's Regiment (Manchester and Liverpool)
	1968	The King's Regiment (8th, 63rd and 96th Foot)
	2006	The Duke of Lancaster's Regiment
63 & 96	1881	The Manchester Regiment
	1958	The King's Regiment (Manchester and Liverpool)
	1967	The King's Regiment (8th, 63rd and 96th)
	2006	The Duke of Lancaster's Regiment

THE ROYAL REGIMENT OF FUSILIERS

5	1881	The Northumberland Fusiliers
	1935	The Royal Northumberland Fusiliers
	1968	The Royal Regiment of Fusiliers
6	1881	The Royal Warwickshire Regiment
	1962	The Royal Warwickshire Fusiliers
	1969	The Royal Regiment of Fusiliers
7	1881	The Royal Fusiliers (City of London Regiment)
	1969	The Royal Regiment of Fusiliers
20	1881	The Lancashire Fusiliers
	1969	The Royal Regiment of Fusiliers

ROYAL ANGLIAN REGIMENT

9	1881	The Norfolk Regiment
	1935	The Royal Norfolk Regiment
	1959	1st East Anglian Regiment (Royal Norfolk and Suffolk)
	1964	Royal Anglian Regiment
12	1881	The Suffolk Regiment
	1959	1st East Anglian Regiment (Royal Norfolk and Suffolk)
	1963	Royal Anglian Regiment
10	1881	The Lincolnshire Regiment
	1946	The Royal Lincolnshire Regiment
	1960	2nd East Anglian Regiment (Duchess of Gloucester's Own Royal Lincolnshire and Northamptonshire)
	1964	Royal Anglian Regiment
48 & 58	1881	The Northamptonshire Regiment
	1961	2nd East Anglian Regiment (Duchess of Gloucester's own Royal Lincolnshire and Northamptonshire)
	1965	Royal Anglian Regiment
16	1881	The Bedfordshire Regiment
	1919	The Bedfordshire and Hertfordshire Regiment
	1958	3rd East Anglian Regiment
	1964	Royal Anglian Regiment
44 & 56	1881	The Essex Regiment
	1958	3rd East Anglian Regiment
	1964	Royal Anglian Regiment
17	1881	The Leicestershire Regiment
	1946	The Royal Leicestershire Regiment
	1964	Royal Anglian Regiment

THE YORKSHIRE REGIMENT

14	1881	The Prince of Wales's Own (West Yorkshire Regiment)
	1920	The West Yorkshire Regiment (Prince of Wales's Own)
	1958	Prince of Wales's Own Regiment of Yorkshire
	2006	1st Battalion, The Yorkshire Regiment
15	1881	The East Yorkshire Regiment
	1935	The East Yorkshire Regiment (Duke of York's Own)
	1958	Prince of Wales's Own Regiment of Yorkshire
	2006	1st Battalion, The Yorkshire Regiment
19	1881	The Princess of Wales's Own (Yorkshire Regiment)

	1902	Alexandra, Princess of Wales's Own Regiment of Yorkshire
	1921	The Green Howards (Alexandra, Princess of Wales's Own Yorkshire Regiment)
	2006	2nd Battalion, The Yorkshire Regiment
33 & 76	1881	The Duke of Wellington's (West Riding Regiment)
	1920	The Duke of Wellington's Regiment (West Riding)
	2006	3rd Battalion, The Yorkshire Regiment

THE MERCIAN REGIMENT

22	1881	The Cheshire Regiment
	2007	1st Battalion, The Mercian Regiment
29 & 36	1881	The Worcestershire Regiment
	1970	The Worcestershire and Sherwood Foresters Regiment
	2007	2nd Battalion, The Mercian Regiment
45 & 95	1881	The Derbyshire Regiment (Sherwood Foresters)
	1902	The Sherwood Foresters (Nottinghamshire and Derbyshire Regiment)
	1971	The Worcestershire and Sherwood Foresters Regiment
	2007	2nd Battalion, The Mercian Regiment
38 & 80	1881	The South Staffordshire Regiment
	1959	The Staffordshire Regiment
	2007	3rd Battalion, The Mercian Regiment
64 & 98	1881	The Prince of Wales's (North Staffordshire Regiment)
	1921	The North Staffordshire Regiment (The Prince of Wales's)
	1959	The Staffordshire Regiment
	2007	3rd Battalion, The Mercian Regiment

THE ROYAL WELSH

23	1881	The Royal Welsh Fusiliers
	1920	The Royal Welch Fusiliers
	2006	1st Battalion, The Royal Welsh
24	1881	The South Wales Borderers
	1969	The Royal Regiment of Wales
	2006	2nd Battalion, The Royal Welsh
41 & 69	1881	The Welch Regiment
	1969	The Royal Regiment of Wales
	2006	2nd Battalion, The Royal Welsh

THE ROYAL IRISH REGIMENT

27 & 108	1881	The Royal Inniskilling Fusiliers
	1968	The Royal Irish Rangers
	1992	The Royal Irish Regiment (on amalgamation with the Ulster Defence Regiment)
83 & 86	1881	The Royal Irish Rifles
	1921	The Royal Ulster Rifles
	1968	The Royal Irish Rangers
	1992	The Royal Irish Regiment (on amalgamation with the Ulster Defence Regiment)
87 & 89	1881	Princess Victoria's (Royal Irish Fusiliers)
	1922	The Royal Irish Fusiliers (Princess Victoria's)
	1968	The Royal Irish Rangers
	1992	The Royal Irish Regiment (on amalgamation with the Ulster Defence Regiment)

THE PARACHUTE REGIMENT

	1942	The Parachute Regiment

THE ROYAL GURKHA RIFLES

	1901	2nd (Prince of Wales's Own) Gurkha Rifles (The Sirmoor Rifles)
	1906	2nd King Edward's Own Gurkha Rifles (The Sirmoor Rifles)
	1936	2nd King Edward VII's Own Gurkha Rifles (The Sirmoor Rifles)
	1994	The Royal Gurkha Rifles
	1902	6th Gurkha Rifles
	1960	6th Queen Elizabeth's Own Gurkha Rifles
	1994	The Royal Gurkha Rifles
	1907	7th Gurkha Rifles
	1961	7th Duke of Edinburgh's Own Gurkha Rifles
	1994	The Royal Gurkha Rifles
	1901	10th Gurkha Rifles
	1949	10th Princess Mary's Own Gurkha Rifles
	1994	The Royal Gurkha Rifles

THE RIFLES

11	1881	The Devonshire Regiment
	1958	The Devonshire and Dorset Regiment
	2007	1st Battalion, The Rifles
39 & 54	1881	The Dorsetshire Regiment
	1959	The Devonshire and Dorset Regiment
	2007	1st Battalion, The Rifles
28 & 81	1881	The Gloucestershire Regiment
	1994	The Royal Gloucestershire, Berkshire and Wiltshire Regiment
	2007	1st Battalion, The Rifles
49 & 66	1881	Princess Charlotte of Wales's (Berkshire Regiment)

	1922	The Royal Berkshire Regiment (Princess Charlotte of Wales's)
	1960	The Duke of Edinburgh's Royal Regiment (Berkshire and Wiltshire)
	1994	The Royal Gloucestershire, Berkshire and Wiltshire Regiment
	2007	1st Battalion, The Rifles

62 & 99	1881	The Duke of Edinburgh's (Wiltshire Regiment)
	1923	The Wiltshire Regiment (Duke of Edinburgh's)
	1961	The Duke of Edinburgh's Royal Regiment (Berkshire and Wiltshire)
	1994	The Royal Gloucestershire, Berkshire and Wiltshire Regiment
	2007	1st Battalion, The Rifles

43 & 52	1881	Oxfordshire Light Infantry
	1908	Oxfordshire and Buckinghamshire Light Infantry
	1958	1st Green Jackets
	1966	The Royal Green Jackets
	2007	2nd and 4th Battalions, The Rifles

60	1881	The King's Royal Rifle Corps
	1928	2nd Green Jackets
	1966	The Royal Green Jackets
	2007	2nd and 4th Battalions, The Rifles

	1881	The Rifle Brigade (Prince Consort's Own)
	1958	3rd Green Jackets
	1966	The Royal Green Jackets
	2007	2nd and 4th Battalions, The Rifles

13	1881	Prince Albert's (Somersetshire Light Infantry)
	1912	Prince Albert's (Somerset Light Infantry)
	1921	The Somerset Light Infantry (Prince Albert's)
	1959	The Somerset and Cornwall Light Infantry
	1968	The Light Infantry
	2007	3rd and 5th Battalions, The Rifles

32 & 46	1881	The Duke of Cornwall's Light Infantry
	1959	The Somerset and Cornwall Light Infantry
	1968	The Light Infantry
	2007	3rd and 5th Battalions, The Rifles

53 & 85	1881	The King's Light Infantry (Shropshire Regiment)
	1882	The King's (Shropshire Light Infantry)
	1920	The King's Shropshire Light Infantry
	1968	The Light Infantry
	2007	3rd and 5th Battalions, The Rifles

51 & 105	1881	The King's Own Light Infantry (South Yorkshire Regiment)
	1887	The King's Own Yorkshire Light Infantry
	1968	The Light Infantry
	2007	3rd and 5th Battalions, The Rifles

68 & 106	1881	The Durham Light Infantry
	1968	The Light Infantry
	2007	3rd and 5th Battalions, The Rifles

SPECIAL AIR SERVICE REGIMENT

	1941	The Special Air Service

DISBANDED REGIMENTS

18	1881	Royal Irish Regiment
	1922	Disbanded
26 & 90	1881	The Cameronians (Scottish Rifles)
	1967	Disbanded
65 & 84	1881	York and Lancaster Regiment
	1968	Suspended animation
88 & 94	1881	The Connaught Rangers
	1922	Disbanded
100 & 109	1881	The Prince of Wales's Leinster Regiment
	1922	Disbanded
101 & 104	1881	The Royal Munster Fusiliers
	1922	Disbanded
102 & 103	1881	The Royal Dublin Fusiliers
	1922	Disbanded

Arms and Services

ROYAL REGIMENT OF ARTILLERY

1881	Royal Regiment of Artillery
1889	Royal Horse Artillery
1889	Royal Field Artillery
1889	Royal Garrison Artillery
1924	Royal Regiment of Artillery

CORPS OF ROYAL ENGINEERS

1881	Corps of Royal Engineers

ROYAL CORPS OF SIGNALS

1920	Corps of Signals
1920	Royal Corps of Signals

ARMY AIR CORPS

1957	Army Air Corps

ROYAL ARMY CHAPLAINS DEPARTMENT

1881	Army Chaplains Department
1919	Royal Army Chaplains Department

103

ROYAL LOGISTIC CORPS

Royal Corps of Transport
1881	Commissariat and Transport Corps
1888	Army Service Corps
1918	Royal Army Service Corps
1965	Royal Corps of Transport
1993	Royal Logistic Corps

Royal Army Ordnance Corps
1881	Ordnance Store Corps
1896	Army Ordnance Corps
1918	Royal Army Ordnance Corps
1993	Royal Logistic Corps

Royal Pioneer Corps
1917	Labour Corps (disbanded **1920**)
1939	Auxiliary Military Pioneer Corps
1940	Pioneer Corps
1946	Royal Pioneer Corps
1993	Royal Logistic Corps

Army Catering Corps
1941	Army Catering Corps
1993	Royal Logistic Corps

ROYAL ARMY MEDICAL CORPS

1884	Medical Staff Corps
1898	Royal Army Medical Corps

ROYAL ARMY VETERINARY CORPS

1881	Army Veterinary Department (Officers)
1903	Army Veterinary Corps (NCOs)
1906	AVD and AVC become Army Veterinary Corps
1918	Royal Army Veterinary Corps

ROYAL ARMY DENTAL CORPS

1926	Army Dental Corps
1946	Royal Army Dental Corps

QUEEN ALEXANDRA'S ROYAL ARMY NURSING CORPS

1881	Army Nursing Service
1887	Princess Christian's Army Nursing Service Reserve
1902	Queen Alexandra's Imperial Military Nursing Service
1949	Queen Alexandra's Royal Army Nursing Corps

ROYAL ELECTRICAL AND MECHANICAL ENGINEERS

1942	Royal Electrical and Mechanical Engineers

ADJUTANT GENERAL'S CORPS

Corps of Royal Military Police
1885	Military Mounted Police and Military Foot Police
1926	Corps of Military Police
1946	Corps of Royal Military Police
1992	Adjutant General's Corps

Military Provost Staff Corps
1901	Military Prison Staff Corps
1906	Military Provost Staff Corps
1992	Adjutant General's Corps

Royal Army Pay Corps
1878	Army Pay Department (officers)
1893	Army Pay Corps (other ranks)
1905	Army Accounts Department
1909	Army Pay Department (1919–27 Corps of Military Accountants)
1920	Royal Army Pay Corps
1992	Adjutant General's Corps

Royal Army Education Corps
1920	Army Education Corps
1946	Royal Army Education Corps
1992	Adjutant General's Corps, Educational and Training Services Branch

Women's Royal Army Corps
1917	Women's Army Auxiliary Corps
	Queen Mary's Army Auxiliary Corps (Disbanded 1921)
	Auxiliary Territorial Service
1949	Women's Royal Army Corps
1992	Adjutant General's Corps

Army Legal Corps
1948	Army Legal Service
1978	Army Legal Corps
1992	Adjutant General's Corps

SMALL ARMS SCHOOL CORPS

1854	School of Musketry
1919	Small Arms School, Hythe
1923	Joined by Machine Gun School, Netheravon
1929	Small Arms School Corps

INTELLIGENCE CORPS

1914	Intelligence Corps

ARMY PHYSICAL TRAINING CORPS

1885	Army Gymnastics Staff
1929	Army Physical Training Staff
1940	Army Physical Training Corps